Kathie Webber's Book of

Summer Cooking

Kathie Webber's Book of
Summer Cooking

ELM TREE BOOKS · LONDON

First published in Great Britain in 1978 by
Elm Tree Books/Hamish Hamilton Ltd
90 Great Russell Street
London WC1B 3PT
and
Sphere Books Ltd
30/32 Gray's Inn Road
London WC1X 8JL

Jacket photograph by Mike Leale
Illustrations by Su Turner

British Library Cataloguing in Publication Data
Webber, Kathie
    Kathie Webber's book of summer cooking.
    1. Cookery
    2. Book of summer cooking
    641.5   TX829

    ISBN 0 241 89819 6

Printed in Great Britain by
Billing & Sons Ltd,
Guildford, Worcester and London

Contents

Introduction   7

Vegetables   9

Salads   32

Starters   43

Fish   58

Meat   78

Fruits   97

Bazaars   113

Drinks   126

Picnics and Barbecues   137

Preserves   153

Index   163

Metric Measurements

Metric measurements may vary from recipe to recipe, and it is essential to follow *either* imperial or metric measures throughout any one recipe. It's perfectly possible to specify 8-oz quantities in two recipes and have one convert to 200 g and the other to 225 g; this is of particular importance with, for example, pastry, where exact quantities are necessary to achieve the correct flour/fat ratio.

Another discrepancy, you may think, occurs when I've specified larger metric amounts of food than one would normally buy by the pound or half-pound. Nowadays we ask for ½ lb of tomatoes, not 7 oz (which may be what we want for a recipe) and in future we shall probably ask for a ½ kilo (kg) rather than 450 g. Half a kilo is a little more than 1 lb, but where the slight difference in weight won't alter the recipe I've given a metric quantity as you'd buy it.

Introduction

Summer Cooking is the second in this series of seasonal books planned and written to help you make the most of the good things that come into the shops and ripen in your gardens during the year. June, July and August are the months when we have our hottest and finest weather, and the varieties of foods available are exciting and immense.

All the soft fruits ripen in the summer – strawberries are quickly followed by raspberries, red and blackcurrants, apricots, peaches and cherries. And though the season for these soft fruits is so very short I think that makes it all the sweeter. Turn them into the most wonderful preserves to eat through the autumn and winter, or enjoy them now and concoct fabulous puddings using lashings of cream, liqueurs, cream cheese and fine sugar. It's the time to be a little extravagant. Those fruits that aren't eaten or those saved from a punnet can be added to cold drinks to be taken into the garden in large frosty jugs. Garnish your drinks by floating sprigs of mint and borage and thin cucumber slices in them as well as perfect specimens of raspberries and strawberries and sprigs of redcurrants. While some of the early varieties of plum are about now, they are really at their best in the autumn months; you'll find exciting ways to prepare both plums and pears in the autumn book.

The big news this season is at the fishmonger rather than the butcher. All the freshwater fish arrives – salmon trout, trout and salmon itself, to be poached gently and served warm with a hollandaise sauce. Lobster and crab make a brief appearance, too, just in time for summer weddings and other special occasions. Halibut, red mullet and prawns help to fill the fishmongers' slabs with colour – all welcome, all good. In contrast, the butcher has little to offer this season that's new. It's almost as if he's resting between the big spring boom and the great autumn fare of game. There's

7

some home-produced veal about though, pink, very tender and with a delicate flavour which should be brought out by simple cooking. It doesn't need smothering in great onion sauces or strong stuffings or too much cream.

Summer is bonanza time at the greengrocers, for along with our home-grown crops of broad beans, corn on the cob, marrows and tomatoes, from abroad come the aubergines, red and green peppers and avocados. And though I've had no luck with avocados in this country, I've very successfully grown aubergines and, slightly less successfully, red peppers, so perhaps soon there'll be more British-grown exotics. Artichokes from France add a Gallic flavour to our cooking and though we under-rate this vegetable, give it a try first and then re-assess it for its place in the kitchen.

Starters take a chapter to themselves in this volume because there are so many – the cold soups made from vegetables, herbs and fruit, the mousses, vegetable water ices, bisques from lobster and crab and the brandade made from salmon.

Herbs, too, are everywhere in the book. If you have a herb garden, these are the months when its yield will be greatest, so make good use of your produce. Make herb butters to top simply-cooked vegetables; add fresh herbs to soured cream, yoghurt, cream cheese and mayonnaise, and use them in soups, sauces, preserves, drinks and puddings.

Summer is the time of the bazaars, fêtes, summer fairs and carnivals and so I've included lots of ideas for the stall that is always popular with the adults – the one piled with home-made foods. Other outdoor activities include picnics, buffets, lunch in the garden, cricket teas and barbecues, and you'll find a whole chapter of ideas for good eating in the open air.

If you enjoyed the *Book of Spring Cooking* I think you'll love this one more – for its wealth of good things from the garden to turn into great things in the kitchen.

KATHIE WEBBER

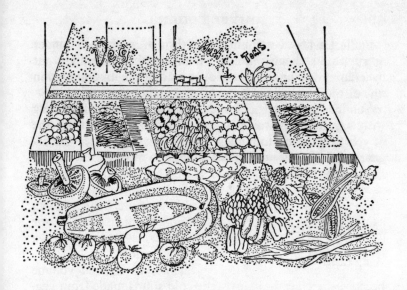

Vegetables

All the summer goodies come in with a rush. Broad beans, the first of the bean family, will, in a month or so, be followed by the runner bean. While they are so young, pick them when the pods are no more than 10 cm (4 in) long and cook them – pods and all – to be served with a herb butter as a vegetable or a starter. Marrows begin to swell and corn on the cob plants grow 'as high as an elephant's eye' with fat, golden fruits.

Of the exotics, globe artichokes can be found in plenty and can be prepared in a number of ways: just as they are, with a vinaigrette dressing; trimmed down into a little cup shape and stuffed; or stripped down entirely to the heart. It's a most versatile vegetable. Aubergines and red and green peppers can be combined with our marvellous tomatoes to make lots of typical Mediterranean dishes such as peperonata, tomato bake and ratatouille. *Imam bayouldi*, from the

Middle East, is a rich aubergine dish over which the Imam is supposed to have fainted. What we shall never know is whether it was the amount of olive oil his wife used to prepare the dish that worried his purse, or whether he simply ate too much of the dish he loved and had digestive troubles. Anyway, try it, but served warm rather than hot or cold. And if you find there's too much oil in it for your taste, you can start off with less, adding just enough to moisten the mixture and cook the aubergines.

Broad Beans

1 kg (2 lb) broad beans   salt

Remove the beans from their pods but don't throw away the pods. Use them to add to a mixed vegetable soup. Bring a large pan of water to the boil, add salt and the beans and cook them for 15 minutes or until tender but not breaking up. Drain well and serve.

Serves 6

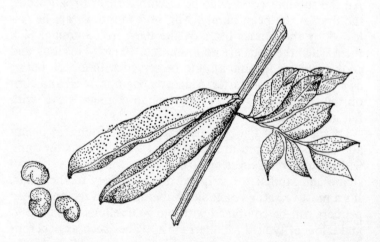

Broad Beans with Parsley Sauce

1 kg (2 lb) broad beans,
  prepared
salt

Parsley sauce:
40 g (1½ oz) butter

40 g (1½ oz) plain flour
375 ml (¾ pint) milk
salt and pepper
30 ml (2 level tablespoons)
  parsley, chopped

Cook the beans in boiling salted water for 15 minutes until tender. Melt the butter in a pan, stir in the flour and cook the roux for 1 minute, then remove it from the heat and gradually stir in the milk. Bring to the boil, stirring all the time, and cook the sauce for 2 minutes. Season well with salt and pepper and stir in the parsley at the last moment before serving. Drain the beans well and pour on the sauce.

Serves 6

Broad Beans with Herb Butter

0·75 kg (1½ lb) broad beans
salt
100 g (4 oz) butter, softened
5 ml (1 level teaspoon)
  chives, chopped

5 ml (1 level teaspoon)
  mint, chopped
10 ml (2 level teaspoons)
  lemon thyme or lemon
  balm, chopped
freshly ground black pepper

Use only very young beans for this dish and pick them when the pods are only 10 cm (4 in) long. Top and tail them, removing any strings from the edges and slice them diagonally into 2·5-cm (1-in) pieces. Drop them into boiling salted water and cook them for 15 minutes or until they are tender but still have a bite to them.

Meanwhile, beat the butter, adding the chives, mint and lemon thyme or balm and just a little salt if the butter is salted (more if you use unsalted butter) and plenty of freshly ground black pepper. Drain the beans well and serve them on small plates with a dollop of herb butter as a first course.

Serves 4

Corn on the Cob

6 corn cobs   75 g (3 oz) butter
salt and pepper

Pull off the outer green leaves and silky fronds from the corn cobs and cut off the stems close to the corn. Bring a very large pan of water to the boil (or use two to give the corn room to move). Add the corn and simmer it for 10 minutes. Don't add salt to the cooking water or overcook corn; both toughen them. Drain and season with salt and pepper and serve with the butter, cutting off pats and letting them melt on the hot corn.

Serves 6

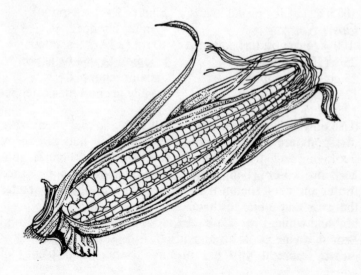

Corn Fritters

6 corn cobs, prepared
200 g (8 oz) plain flour
salt and pepper
2 large egg yolks
250 ml ($\frac{1}{2}$ pint) cider

oil for deep frying
1 large lemon
10 ml (2 level teaspoons)
  mint, chopped

Cook the cobs in plenty of boiling unsalted water for 10 minutes, then test to see if you can remove the kernels easily by scraping. If not, cook for a couple more minutes. Allow to cool, then remove the kernels with a sharp knife.

Sift the flour with a good pinch each of salt and pepper. Make a well in the centre and add the yolks and cider and beat to a smooth batter. Combine the corn and the batter and drop this mixture from a 15-ml spoon (1 tablespoon) into deep hot fat. Fry until golden and drain on kitchen paper. Cut the lemon into wedges. Arrange the corn fritters on a plate, garnish with lemon and sprinkle with mint.

Makes 20

Corn Soufflé

25 g (1 oz) butter
25 g (1 oz) plain flour
125 ml ($\frac{1}{4}$ pint) milk
125 ml ($\frac{1}{4}$ pint) single cream
0·5 kg (1 lb) corn kernels
  (see above)

3 large eggs, separated
salt and pepper
ground nutmeg
1 large egg white

Melt the butter in a pan, stir in the flour and cook the roux for 1 minute. Remove from the heat and gradually stir in the milk and cream to make a smooth sauce. Bring to the boil and simmer for 2 minutes, then stir in the corn kernels. Beat in the egg yolks and salt and pepper and ground nutmeg to season well. Whisk the egg whites until stiff but not dry and fold them into the slightly cooled mixture. Pour at once into a greased 15-cm (6-in) soufflé dish. Bake at 200°C (400°F)/Gas 6 for about 30 minutes or until the soufflé is risen and golden brown.

Serves 4

Perfectly Cooked Marrow

1 large marrow   ground mace
salt and pepper

Peel the marrow, cut it in half lengthwise and scoop out the seeds using a sharp knife. Cut the flesh into 2·5-cm (1-in) cubes. Put them in the top of a steamer and steam for 25–30 minutes until cooked but not soft and squashy. Turn on to a serving dish and sprinkle with salt, pepper and ground mace before serving.

Serves 6

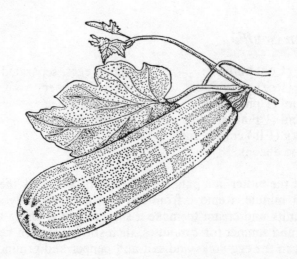

Marrow with Lemon Sauce

1 medium-sized marrow,
  cubed

Lemon sauce:
50 g (2 oz) butter
3 large egg yolks
125 ml (¼ pint) single
  cream

salt and pepper
5 ml (1 level teaspoon)
  lemon rind, finely grated
15 ml (1 tablespoon) lemon
  juice, strained
15 ml (1 level tablespoon)
  parsley, finely chopped

Put the marrow in the top of a steamer and steam it for 25–30 minutes until cooked but not too soft.

Gently heat the butter for the sauce. Beat the egg yolks and cream together and stir into the butter, seasoning the mixture well with salt and pepper. Heat the sauce very slowly over a low heat until it thickens. If you let it boil it will curdle and spoil. Stir in the lemon rind and juice and parsley and serve at once poured over the marrow.

Serves 4–6

Smothered Marrow

1 medium-sized marrow

Mustard sauce:
25 g (1 oz) butter
25 g (1 oz) plain flour
250 ml (½ pint) milk

15 ml (1 level tablespoon)
  mustard powder
salt and pepper
50 g (2 oz) fresh white
  breadcrumbs
25 g (1 oz) butter

Peel the marrow and cut it into thin slices. Scoop the seeds out of the centres and arrange the marrow rings in a shallow baking dish. Melt 25 g (1 oz) butter for the sauce and stir in the flour. Cook the mixture for 1 minute, then remove from the heat and stir in the milk. Bring to the boil and stir in the mustard and salt and pepper. Pour this sauce over the marrow.

Sprinkle the surface with breadcrumbs and dot with the remaining butter. Bake at 200°C (400°F)/Gas 6 for 30 minutes until the top is golden brown.

Serves 4–6

Artichokes Vinaigrette

6 globe artichokes
salt

Vinaigrette:
5 ml (1 level teaspoon)
   mustard powder
salt and pepper

15 ml (1 tablespoon)
   vinegar
60 ml (4 tablespoons)
   olive or good salad oil
1 small onion, finely
   chopped
1 clove garlic, crushed
celery seeds

Choose globe artichokes that have tight fleshy leaves – ones that look fresh, not dried and dusty. Cut off the stems close to the base of the leaves and remove any dry and discoloured outer leaves. After washing in plenty of cold water, leave them soaking for 30 minutes to remove any dirt between the close-packed leaves. Drain well, drop them into fast-boiling salted water and cook until the leaves will pull away easily – this will take anything from 20 minutes to 1 hour depending on the size and the age of the artichoke and how long it was sitting in the greengrocers before you picked it. Remove and leave to drain upside down.

For the vinaigrette, blend the mustard and a good pinch each of salt and pepper with the vinegar. Whisk in the oil, then stir in the onion, garlic and a pinch of celery seeds and leave to stand for 30 minutes before using. If liked, strain this vinaigrette before pouring some over each artichoke.

Eat a globe artichoke by pulling off a leaf at a time, dipping the fleshy base of each one in vinaigrette and then sucking. When you get to the centre, remove the frondy top (called the choke), cutting just where the fronds join and become a solid base. It's this base, the artichoke bottom or heart, that is considered the great delicacy. Eat it with a knife and fork and the remaining vinaigrette.

Serves 6

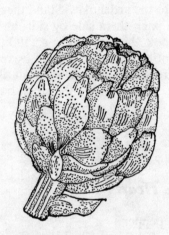 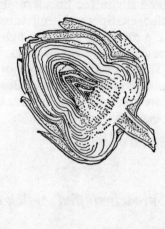

Stuffed Artichokes

6 medium-sized globe
   artichokes
juice of 1 lemon, strained
1 small onion, finely
   chopped
100 g (4 oz) mushrooms,
   chopped
15 ml (1 tablespoon)
   cooking oil

15 ml (1 level tablespoon)
   fresh white breadcrumbs
salt and pepper
30 ml (2 level tablespoons)
   parsley, finely chopped
100 g (4 oz) cooked
   chicken, finely chopped
500 ml (1 pint) chicken
   stock

Remove any discoloured outer leaves from the artichokes and cut off the stalks. Cut off a third from the top of each artichoke and dip the cut leaves at once in lemon juice to prevent them browning. Snip off the points of the remaining leaves with scissors and dip again in lemon juice. Pull out the small inner leaves close to the centre and, using a teaspoon, remove the choke, the frondy centre. Sprinkle lemon juice over the exposed hearts. Press the leaves together again to make a good cup shape.

Fry the onion and mushrooms in the oil for 5 minutes, then stir in the breadcrumbs, salt and pepper, parsley and chicken. Spoon this mixture into the artichokes. Stand them in a meat tin, small enough to pack them side by side, and pour in the chicken stock. Cook the artichokes at 190°C (375°F)/Gas 5 for 1 hour or until one of the bottom leaves can be pulled out easily. Baste regularly with the stock until, towards the end of the cooking time, most of the stock has been absorbed. Serve hot.

Serves 6

Spinach-stuffed Artichoke Hearts

4 large artichokes
juice of 1 lemon, strained
salt
0·5 kg (1 lb) spinach,
    prepared
60 ml (4 tablespoons)
    double cream

pepper
25 g (1 oz) Cheddar
    cheese, grated
25 g (1 oz) Parmesan
    cheese, grated

Break off the outer artichoke leaves, then cut off the stems close to the base. Cut off the remaining leaves, including the frondy choke just above the heart. Rub the hearts with lemon juice, then cut off the ends of the leaves remaining round the sides. Coat again with lemon juice to prevent the hearts browning. Cook them in plenty of boiling salted water for 20 to 30 minutes until just tender.

Meanwhile, put the spinach in a pan with just the water clinging to the leaves after washing and cook for 15 minutes.

Drain off any excess water and blend by chopping with the cream to make a purée. Season with salt and pepper. Arrange the drained hearts in a baking dish just large enough to hold them in one layer, and spoon the spinach into the centre of each one. Mix the cheeses and sprinkle them over the spinach. Bake at 180°C (350°F)/Gas 4 for 10 minutes until golden brown on top. These make a small but delicious starter.

Serves 4

Ratatouille

2 large green peppers
2 medium-sized aubergines
0·5 kg (1 lb) ripe tomatoes

3 large courgettes
90 ml (6 tablespoons) olive oil
1 clove garlic, crushed
salt and pepper

Rinse all the vegetables but don't peel any of them, simply remove the stalks. Cut the peppers in half, remove the cores, white pithy membranes and seeds. Cut the peppers, aubergines, tomatoes and courgettes into even-sized chunks. Heat the oil in a heavy frying pan (or two) and add the vegetables and garlic. Cook quite quickly for 15 minutes, stirring frequently, then lower the heat and simmer until the mixture is soft, seasoning well with salt and pepper at this time. When cooked, check the seasoning and serve hot or cold as a starter or a salad, or hot as a vegetable with plain roasts or steaks. You might like to add a good sprinkling of grated Parmesan or other cheese if the ratatouille is to be a first course.

Serves 4

Peperonata

2 large onions, sliced
25 g (1 oz) butter
45 ml (3 tablespoons)
   olive oil

8 large red peppers,
   prepared
8 large ripe tomatoes
1 clove garlic, crushed
salt and pepper

Fry the onion in the mixture of butter and olive oil for 5 minutes. Cut the prepared peppers into strips, add them to the pan, lower the heat and simmer slowly for 30–40 minutes or until the peppers are soft. Drop the tomatoes into lots of boiling water and when the skins split, remove and peel them off. Chop the tomatoes and add them to the peppers together with the garlic and plenty of salt and pepper and simmer again until cooked. Serve hot as a vegetable or cold as a starter or a salad.

Serves 6

Stuffed Peppers

4 large peppers
1 large onion, finely
  chopped
25 g (1 oz) butter
4 rashers streaky bacon,
  chopped
100 g (4 oz) long-grain rice

15 ml (1 tablespoon)
  tomato paste
10 ml (2 level teaspoons)
  basil, chopped
salt and pepper
500 ml (1 pint) good
  chicken stock

Slice the tops off the peppers and remove the seeds and membranes, being careful to keep the peppers whole. Reserve the tops, but take off any stalks. Fry the onion in the butter with the bacon and rice for 5 minutes. Stir in the tomato paste, basil and salt and pepper. Add 250 ml ($\frac{1}{2}$ pint) stock and simmer the mixture for 15 minutes until the stock has been absorbed. Spoon this mixture into the peppers and put on the tops. Stand them in a dish which is just large enough to hold them upright during baking. Pour the remaining stock round the peppers. Bake them at 190°C (375°F)/Gas 5 for about 30–45 minutes or until the peppers themselves are cooked, basting them occasionally with the stock. Serve with a little of the stock poured over them.

Serves 4

Tagliatelle Napoletana

1 kg (2 lb) ripe tomatoes,
  skinned
1 clove garlic, crushed
60 ml (4 tablespoons) olive
  oil

salt and pepper
5 ml (1 level teaspoon)
  oregano, chopped
0·5 kg (1 lb) tagliatelle

To make the tomato sauce, chop the tomatoes, discarding the seeds. Put the flesh with the garlic and olive oil in a heavy pan and season the mixture with salt and pepper.

Simmer the sauce for 30 minutes or so over a medium heat until it is thick. Stir in the oregano just before serving.

Toss the tagliatelle into a large pan of boiling salted water and cook it for about 12 minutes or until soft but not squashy if you press a piece between finger and thumb. Drain well and toss in the sauce until the pasta is well coated. Serve at once.

Serves 6

Tomato Bake

4 red peppers, prepared	1 clove garlic, crushed
	10 ml (2 level teaspoons)
Tomato sauce:	basil, chopped
0·5 kg (1 lb) ripe tomatoes, chopped	salt and pepper
30 ml (2 tablespoons) olive oil	75 g (3 oz) Cheddar cheese, sliced

When you prepare the peppers, cut them in half lengthwise and arrange the halves, skin side upwards, on a grill pan. Grill until the skin blackens and blisters, let them cool and then rub off the skins. Arrange the halves, cut side up, in one layer in a baking dish. Cook the tomatoes in the olive oil with the garlic for 30 minutes or until they soften almost to a paste. Remove any coarse pieces of skin, stir in the basil and season well with salt and pepper. Spoon this tomato sauce into each pepper half and bake them at 180°C (350°F)/Gas 4 for 5 minutes, then cover them with the cheese slices and return to the oven until the cheese has melted. Serve hot.

Serves 4

Stuffed Tomatoes

6 large tomatoes
50 g (2 oz) fresh white
   breadcrumbs
15 ml (1 tablespoon)
   cooking oil
few sprigs of basil

¼ cucumber, peeled
50 g (2 oz) cream cheese
5 ml (1 level teaspoon)
   marjoram, chopped
50 g (2 oz) peeled shrimps
salt and pepper

Cut the tops off the tomatoes (you can leave the stalks in place) and scoop out and discard the seeds. Reserve the tops. Fry the breadcrumbs in the hot oil with the basil sprigs, stirring them round until they are crisp and golden. Drain on kitchen paper and discard the basil. Chop the cucumber into small dice. Beat the cream cheese until it is soft, then beat in the cucumber, marjoram and peeled shrimps. Season well with pepper but watch the salt because the shrimps may well be slightly salty. Pack this mixture into the tomato cases and top with the crisp breadcrumbs. Add the tomato lids and serve with salads or cold meats. If you aren't going to serve them immediately, don't add the bread-crumbs. They soften if kept standing so add them at the last moment.

Serves 6

Runner Beans

0·5 kg (1 lb) runner beans   pepper
salt   25 g (1 oz) butter

Top and tail the runner beans and remove any strings from
the sides. Cut the beans into narrow diagonal slices. Drop
the slices into plenty of boiling salted water and cook them
for 10 minutes or until tender but still slightly crisp. Drain
well and sprinkle with plenty of pepper, preferably freshly
ground, and put a huge knob of butter on top before sending
them to table.

Serves 4

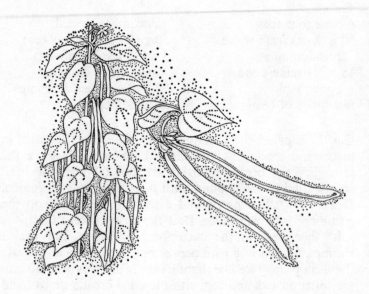

Runner Beans with Chive Sauce

0·5 kg (1 lb) runner beans, sliced
salt
125 ml (¼ pint) natural yoghurt
15 ml (1 level tablespoon) chives, snipped
5 ml (1 teaspoon) lemon juice, strained
5 ml (1 level teaspoon) lemon rind, finely grated
pepper

Cook the beans in plenty of boiling salted water for 10 minutes until tender but still crisp. Whisk the yoghurt with the chives, lemon juice and rind and season it with salt and pepper. Drain the beans well and top each portion with a few spoons of the sauce.

Serves 4

Runner Beans Kassandra

0·75 kg (1½ lb) runner beans, sliced
salt
90 ml (6 tablespoons) olive oil
1 large onion, roughly chopped
0·5 kg (1 lb) ripe tomatoes, skinned
30 ml (2 level tablespoons) oregano, chopped
pepper
15 ml (1 level tablespoon) parsley, chopped
pinch of caster sugar

Put the beans in a colander and sprinkle them with plenty of salt. Leave them for 1 hour or so to soften, then rinse well. Before you continue with this dish, taste a piece of bean to make sure you've washed off all the salt. Ideally, soak the beans in fresh water for 10 minutes to make sure. Dry the beans, then put them in a large heavy pan with the olive oil and onion. Chop the tomatoes and add to the pan with the oregano and plenty of pepper. Simmer the beans for 25–30 minutes until they are tender. The beans in this recipe can be cooked until they are fairly soft but make sure the sauce is thick before you finish cooking. Stir in the parsley and caster sugar and serve warm with crusty bread.

Serves 4

Fried Aubergines

4 medium-sized aubergines	60 ml (4 tablespoons)
salt	olive oil
plain flour	15 ml (1 level tablespoon)
50 g (2 oz) butter	parsley, coarsely chopped
	black pepper

Rinse the aubergines and cut off the stems and small surrounding green leaves. Slice the aubergines into 1·25-cm (½-in) rounds. Layer them in a colander, sprinkling each layer with salt, then put a small plate on top (small enough to go inside the colander) and weight it. Leave to stand for 1 hour. Aubergines have quite a lot of liquid in them and it can be bitter. Treat them like this and you won't find that your dishes contain a curious metallic taste that can't be traced. Rinse the aubergines well to remove all the salt and dry them on kitchen paper. Dust each slice with flour.

Heat the butter and oil in batches in a frying pan and fry the aubergines a few at a time until golden brown on both sides. Drain on kitchen paper and keep warm as you cook the rest. Pile them on a serving plate and sprinkle with the parsley and some black pepper.

Serves 4

Baked Cheesy Aubergines

1 kg (2 lb) aubergines,
  sliced
salt
olive oil
1 large onion, chopped
0·5 kg (1 lb) ripe tomatoes,
  skinned
1 clove garlic, crushed

few sprigs of basil
pepper
plain flour
100 g (4 oz) Cheddar
  cheese, grated
50 g (2 oz) Parmesan
  cheese, grated

Layer the aubergine slices in a colander, sprinkling each layer
with plenty of salt, then put a small plate on top (small
enough to fit inside the colander) and weight the plate.
Leave the aubergines for 1 hour to drain.

Heat 30 ml (2 tablespoons) olive oil in a frying pan and fry
the onion for 5 minutes, then chop the tomatoes and add
them to the pan with the garlic and basil sprigs. Stir and
cook for about 20 minutes until the tomatoes become a
thick sauce. Season with salt and plenty of black pepper.
Rinse the aubergines to remove the salt and dry them on
kitchen paper. Lightly flour both sides of each slice and fry

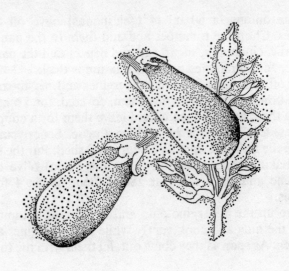

them a few at a time in hot olive oil, using 30 ml (2 table-spoons) each time, until golden on both sides. Drain on kitchen paper.

Put a layer of aubergines in a baking dish and sprinkle with some of the mixed cheeses. Add some sauce and continue layering the ingredients, finishing with a small sprinkle of cheese on top of a layer of sauce. Bake at 180°C (350°F)/ Gas 4 for about 40 minutes until golden on top.

Serves 6

Imam Bayouldi

225 g (½ lb) onions, chopped	pinch of caster sugar
olive oil	salt and pepper
0·5 kg (1 lb) tomatoes, skinned	30 ml (2 level tablespoons) parsley, finely chopped
1 clove garlic, crushed	4 medium-sized aubergines
pinch of ground cinnamon	25 g (1 oz) almonds, finely chopped

Fry the onions in 60 ml (4 tablespoons) olive oil for 5 minutes. Chop the tomatoes and add them to the pan with the garlic, cinnamon, sugar, salt and pepper and the parsley. Simmer for 30 minutes until the mixture is thick.

Cut off the stalks from the aubergines and put them in a pan of boiling water and cook them, covered, for 5 minutes. Plunge them into cold water and leave them for a couple of minutes. Cut each one in half lengthwise. Scoop out and reserve the flesh, leaving a 1·25-cm (½-in) shell. Put the shells on a baking tray, pour 15 ml (1 tablespoon) olive oil in each one and bake them at 180°C (350°F)/Gas 4 for 15 minutes.

Chop up the aubergine pulp and add it to the tomatoes, stir in the nuts and cook gently while the aubergines are in the oven. As soon as they come out, fill them with the tomato mixture, return them to the oven and cook them for another 30 minutes. Allow to cool to room temperature before eating.

Serves 4–6

Creamed Mushrooms on Toast

225 g (8 oz) mushrooms
75 g (3 oz) butter
40 g (1½ oz) plain flour
375 ml (¾ pint) milk

salt and pepper
4 slices white bread, toasted

Rinse and dry the mushrooms; there is no need to peel them. Cut them into quarters or halves if large. Melt the butter in a large saucepan and fry the mushrooms for 5 minutes, turning them all the time. Stir in the flour and cook the mixture gently for 1 minute. Remove from the heat and gradually stir in the milk, then bring the sauce to the boil, stirring. Simmer gently for 3 or 4 minutes and season the mushrooms well with salt and pepper. Pile on to hot toast and serve at once for suppers or as a snack.

The big flat mushrooms colour this sauce almost the same shade as their gills and the flavour is marvellous, but if this doesn't appeal to you, use the tiny button variety.

Serves 4

Mushroom Fritters

Fritter batter:
100 g (4 oz) plain flour
pinch of salt
15 ml (1 tablespoon)
    cooking oil
125 ml (¼ pint) warm water
1 large egg white, whisked

100 g (4 oz) open cap
    mushrooms
oil for deep frying
1 large lemon
15 ml (1 level tablespoon)
    parsley, finely chopped

Sift together the flour and salt and make a well in the centre.
Add the oil and water and beat well to make a smooth batter.
Fold in the egg white and use immediately.

Trim each mushroom stalk to about 1·25 cm (½ in) and
dip the mushrooms in the batter. Shake off the excess and
lower into fat hot enough to fry a cube of bread golden in 1
minute. Fry until golden brown, then drain on kitchen paper.
Cut the lemon into wedges. Arrange the fritters on a serving
dish, surround with the lemon wedges and sprinkle with
parsley.

Serves 4

Mushroom Tartlets

Rich shortcrust pastry:
225 g (8 oz) plain flour
pinch of salt
100 g (4 oz) butter
50 g (2 oz) lard
1 egg yolk

Béchamel sauce:
25 g (1 oz) butter

25 g (1 oz) plain flour
250 ml (½ pint) milk
225 g (8 oz) mushrooms,
    chopped
salt and pepper
45 ml (3 tablespoons)
    double cream
10 ml (2 level teaspoons)
    thyme, chopped

Sift the flour and salt into a bowl and rub in the fats. Mix
to a stiff dough with the egg yolk and 30 ml (2 tablespoons)

cold water. Roll the pastry on a lightly floured board and use to line eight 10-cm (4-in) tartlet tins. Prick the base of each tartlet, line with greaseproof paper and fill with baking beans. Bake them at 200°C (400°F)/Gas 6 for about 10 minutes, then remove the beans and paper and bake them for 5 minutes more or until golden brown.

Meanwhile, make the béchamel sauce. Melt the butter in a pan, stir in the flour and cook the mixture for 1 minute. Remove from the heat and gradually stir in the milk, then bring to the boil and cook, stirring, for 2 minutes. Stir in the mushrooms and cook them for 2 minutes then season well with salt and pepper. Stir in the cream and thyme, spoon into the cases and serve hot.

Serves 8

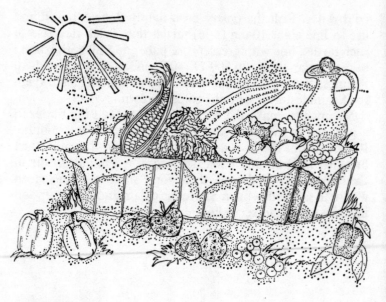

Salads

Summer is perhaps the biggest season for salads, with all the different varieties of vegetables available to make the standard combination of lettuce, cucumber and radishes much more interesting. Broad beans and runner beans both make tasty dishes while sweetcorn and red and green peppers add colour. Artichokes, stripped of their leaves, reveal the heart which is a great delicacy and, married with mushrooms, a great treat. Sadly, there is no use for the discarded leaves when you make artichoke-heart salads but I find them well worth the expense involved.

Salade Niçoise from France, cucumber mint raita from India and a Greek fish salad provide different combinations of ingredients from those we're familiar with. Include chicken and fish in your salads to make main meals of them rather than side dishes, and experiment by adding various summer fruits.

Avocado Salad

225 g (8 oz) haricot beans,   1 large onion, sliced
   cooked   2 large avocados
4 rashers streaky bacon,   30 ml (2 tablespoons)
   chopped   lemon juice, strained
113-g (4-oz) can tuna fish,   vinaigrette (see page 16)
   drained

Put the beans in a large mixing bowl. Fry the bacon pieces
until they are really crisp, then drain them on kitchen paper.
Flake the tuna and add to the beans with the onion slices
separated into rings. Using a stainless steel knife, peel the
avocados, cut them in half and remove the stones. Cut the
flesh into 2·5-cm (1-in) chunks. Toss at once in the lemon
juice to prevent them turning brown. Strain the vinaigrette,
add to the beans and tuna with the avocado and toss gently
to mix. Sprinkle with the bacon pieces and serve at once
before the bacon loses its crispness.

Serves 6

Bean Salad Starter

0·5 kg (1 lb) runner beans,   1 red pepper, prepared
   prepared   2 hard-boiled eggs, shelled
salt   vinaigrette (see page 16)
50 g (2 oz) black olives

When you prepare the beans, slice them across instead of
diagonally, then cook them in boiling salted water for 10
minutes until tender but still crisp. Drain well and mix with
the black olives. Cut the red pepper into thin slices and cut
the eggs into six wedges lengthwise. Stir the pepper into the
beans and pour on the vinaigrette. Toss the salad and garnish
with the hard-boiled eggs.

Serves 4

Salad of Artichoke Hearts

24 artichoke hearts, cooked
1 large onion, sliced
2 rashers streaky bacon

100 g (4 oz) canned red
  beans, drained
vinaigrette (see page 16)

Leave small artichoke hearts whole but slice large ones into
quarters. Separate the onion slices into rings and mix with
the artichoke pieces. Remove the rinds from the bacon and
chop the rashers. Fry the rinds until the fat runs, then fry
the bacon pieces and rinds together until they are crisp.
Stir the canned beans and the vinaigrette into the artichokes
and garnish with the bacon pieces. Crisp crushed bacon rinds
sprinkled on this salad will add to the flavour.

Serves 4

Corn Salad

0·5 kg (1 lb) corn kernels
  (see page 13)
1 large green pepper,
  chopped
1 large onion, roughly
  chopped

15 ml (1 tablespoon)
  vinegar
5 ml (1 level teaspoon)
  chives, snipped
5 ml (1 level teaspoon)
  parsley, chopped
salt and pepper

Garlic herb dressing:
30 ml (2 tablespoons)
  single cream
1 clove garlic, crushed
30 ml (2 tablespoons) salad
  oil

Croûtons:
2 slices white bread
45 ml (3 tablespoons) oil

Combine the corn kernels, green pepper and onion in a bowl.
Whisk the cream, garlic, oil and vinegar for the dressing, then
stir in the herbs and season with salt and pepper. Toss the
corn in this dressing and transfer it to a serving dish. Cut
the crusts off the bread and dice the slices. Fry in hot oil

until golden brown, stirring all the time. Drain well. Sprinkle the croûtons over the salad.

Serves 4–6

Marinated Mushrooms

225 g (8 oz) button
  mushrooms, sliced
3 ml (½ teaspoon) mustard
  powder
1 clove garlic, crushed

125 ml (¼ pint) cider
  vinegar
5 ml (1 teaspoon) tabasco
  sauce
salt and pepper

Put the mushrooms in a serving dish. Whisk together the mustard, garlic, vinegar, tabasco sauce and salt and pepper to taste. Pour over the mushrooms and leave them to marinate for 8 hours. Drain and serve sprinkled with chives.

Serves 4

Green Peppers Mix

2 large green peppers
3 large tomatoes, sliced
8 spring onions, sliced

Dressing:
5 ml (1 level teaspoon)
  made mustard

10 ml (2 teaspoons) white
  wine vinegar
45 ml (3 tablespoons) olive
  oil
salt and pepper
celery seeds

Arrange rings of pepper with tomato slices and sprinkle with spring onion.

Blend the mustard with the vinegar, then whisk in the oil. Season the dressing and add a pinch of celery seeds. Pour over the peppers, leave for 30 minutes, then serve.

Serves 4

Broad Bean Salad

0·5 kg (1 lb) broad beans,
  cooked
25 g (1 oz) fennel root,
  chopped

½ box mustard and cress,
  prepared
vinaigrette (see page 16)
5 ml (1 level teaspoon)
  thyme, chopped

Gently mix the beans, chopped fennel and mustard and cress. Strain the vinaigrette (after letting it stand for 30 minutes) and pour it over the salad. Sprinkle with the thyme and serve immediately.

Serves 4

Tomato Salad

1 kg (2 lb) tomatoes,
  skinned
1 large onion, finely
  chopped

15 ml (1 level tablespoon)
  parsley, finely chopped
vinaigrette (see page 16)

Slice the tomatoes and arrange them on a serving dish. Sprinkle with the onion and parsley, and pour on the vinaigrette. Leave for at least 30 minutes before serving.

Serves 8

Cucumber Mint Raita

½ small cucumber, peeled
142-g (5-oz) carton plain
  yoghurt
1 small onion, finely
  chopped

½ small green pepper,
  finely chopped
salt and pepper
10 ml (2 level teaspoons)
  mint, chopped

Cut the cucumber into small dice and mix it with the yoghurt. Stir in the onion, green pepper, plenty of salt and pepper and the mint. Serve at once.

Serves 2–4

Artichoke Mushroom Hearts

4 large artichoke hearts or
   8 medium-sized ones,
   prepared
juice of 1 lemon, strained
salt

100 g (4 oz) button
   mushrooms
vinaigrette (see page 16)
15 ml (1 level tablespoon)
   thyme, chopped

As soon as you have prepared the artichoke hearts, coat them with the lemon juice to prevent them browning, then cook them in plenty of boiling salted water for 20 minutes until tender but still firm. Drain and allow to cool completely. Rinse the mushrooms and slice them finely, slicing the stalks as well.

Arrange the hearts on 4 plates and cover them with the mushroom slices, making a pattern of the overlapping pieces. Pour on the vinaigrette and sprinkle with the chopped thyme.

Serves 4

Greek Fish Salad

0·5 kg (1 lb) red mullet,
   filleted
½ small onion, chopped
1 large lemon
1 bay leaf
6 peppercorns

60 ml (4 tablespoons) olive
   oil
salt and pepper
15 ml (1 level tablespoon)
   parsley, finely chopped
15 ml (1 level tablespoon)
   oregano, finely chopped

Rinse the fish fillets and put them in a large pan with the onion. Peel off a strip of lemon rind (without any pith on it) and add it to the pan with the bay leaf and peppercorns. Pour in 500 ml (1 pint) cold water and bring gently to the boil, then simmer for 10 minutes. Don't cook the fish longer because it breaks up too much. Remove from the liquid and allow to cool. When cool enough to handle, remove any bones and large pieces of skin and flake the fish into large pieces.

Whisk the oil with plenty of salt and pepper and the parsley and oregano. Put the fish into 4 serving dishes and pour over the oil. Cut some slices of lemon to use as a garnish.

Serves 4

Peachy Salad

1 small lettuce, prepared
225 g (8 oz) cottage cheese
15 ml (1 level tablespoon)
  chives, snipped
salt and pepper

4 large peaches, sliced
50 g (2 oz) redcurrants,
  prepared
142-g (5-oz) carton soured
  cream

Arrange the lettuce leaves on a large serving dish. Stir the cottage cheese with the chives and plenty of salt and freshly ground black pepper to mix and pile it in the centre of the plate. Arrange the peach slices on the cottage cheese. Put the redcurrants in a small pan, add 30 ml (2 tablespoons) cold water and simmer them very gently until the first currant bursts. Remove them from the heat immediately and cool. When cold, drain them and fold them into the soured cream, spoon over the peaches and serve at once.

Serves 4–6

Salade Niçoise

0·75 kg (1½ lb) runner
  beans, prepared
salt
1 clove garlic, crushed
0·5 kg (1 lb) ripe
  tomatoes, quartered

20 black olives
198-g (7-oz) can tuna,
  drained
3 hard-boiled eggs, shelled
12 anchovy fillets
vinaigrette (see page 16)

Use young runner beans for this recipe, not more than
10 cm (4 in) long, and cook them whole in boiling salted
water for about 10 minutes until cooked but still crisp to
bite. Drain and leave to cool. Stir the garlic with the tomatoes, olives and tuna and mix with the cold beans. Cut the
hard-boiled eggs into wedges and add with the anchovies.
Pour the strained vinaigrette over the salad.

Serves 4–6

Shrimp and Grapefruit Salad

1 small lettuce, prepared
1 grapefruit
½ cucumber, peeled
225 g (8 oz) peeled shrimps

Mayonnaise:
1 large egg yolk

salt and pepper
good pinch of mustard
  powder
125 ml (¼ pint) salad oil
5 ml (1 teaspoon) lemon
  juice, strained
15 ml (1 tablespoon) hot
  water

Arrange the lettuce leaves on 4 small plates. Using a sharp
knife, peel the grapefruit, removing all the pith at the same
time. Hold the peeled fruit in one hand and make a sharp
downward cut between one segment and the skin, then
another between the skin and the segment on the other
side of it. Cut the flesh out and drop it into a bowl. Continue
in this way until you are left with just the skins. Squeeze

them to remove all the juice. Chop the cucumber into small dice. Rinse the shrimps. Chop the grapefruit segments into 3 or 4 pieces depending on their size and mix them with the cucumber and shrimps.

Blend the egg yolk in a bowl with a good pinch each of salt and pepper and the mustard. Gradually add the oil, drop by drop at first, beating all the time. As the mixture thickens and you have incorporated about half the oil, you'll find you can speed up a little but if at any time the mayonnaise looks like curdling, stop adding oil and beat furiously. If it *does* curdle, take another egg yolk and gradually beat the mayonnaise into it. When the texture looks right again, add the remaining oil. Beat in the lemon juice and hot water and check the seasoning. Stir some of the

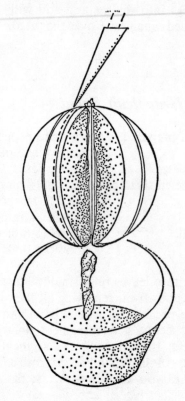

mayonnaise into the grapefruit and shrimps and turn gently to coat. Season the salad with salt and pepper and pile it on the lettuce. Serve the remaining mayonnaise in a bowl.

Serves 4

Fruity Crunch

1 cucumber, peeled
2 celery stalks, thinly sliced
1 cooking apple, diced
2 large peaches, sliced
4 apricots, chopped
50 g (2 oz) seedless raisins

50 g (2 oz) unsalted peanuts
mayonnaise (see page 40)
30 ml (2 tablespoons) double cream
15 ml (1 level tablespoon) parsley, chopped

Chop the cucumber into small dice and mix with the celery, apple, peaches, apricots, raisins and peanuts. Blend the mayonnaise with the double cream and gently mix into the salad. Sprinkle with the parsley and serve at once.

Serves 4–6

Salmon Salad

175 g (6 oz) long-grain rice
salt
225 g (8 oz) salmon tail
few parsley stalks
1 bay leaf
1 blade of mace
8 radishes
1 large lemon

60 ml (4 tablespoons) double cream
60 ml (4 tablespoons) mayonnaise (see page 40)
30 ml (2 tablespoons) tomato paste
pepper

Cook the rice in plenty of boiling salted water for 12 minutes. Rinse the fish and put it in a pan with the parsley stalks, bay leaf and mace. Just cover the fish with cold water, bring slowly to the boil and simmer for 10 minutes. Lift it on to a plate and when it is cool enough to handle, remove the skin and bones and flake the fish into small pieces. Drain the rice and rinse it under running cold water.

Cut off the roots and stalks from the radishes and cut them into thin slices. Finely grate the rind from the lemon and squeeze out and strain the juice. Whisk the double cream to the soft peak stage and fold it gently into the mayonnaise with the tomato paste. Season it with salt and pepper, the lemon rind and juice. Mix the rice with the salmon and radishes and gently fold in the rosy mayonnaise, turning everything gently to coat with the dressing. Press the mixture into a mould, smooth the surface and leave it in the fridge for 3 hours to chill. Turn on to a plate to serve and garnish with leaves of lettuce from the heart and with cucumber slices.

Serves 8

Strawberry Chicken Salad

225 g (8 oz) long-grain rice
salt
100 g (4 oz) peas, shelled
225 g (8 oz) cooked
  chicken

225 g (8 oz) small
  strawberries, hulled
90 ml (6 tablespoons)
  mayonnaise (see page 40)
pepper

Rinse the rice and cook it for 12 minutes in plenty of boiling salted water. Cook the peas in boiling salted water for 20 minutes. Drain the cooked rice and rinse it under running cold water. Drain and similarly rinse the peas. Cut the chicken into pieces and mix it with the rice and peas. Halve or quarter the strawberries depending on their size. Mix into the rice with the mayonnaise and salt and pepper, turning it over carefully to mix the salad without breaking up the ingredients.

Serves 6–8

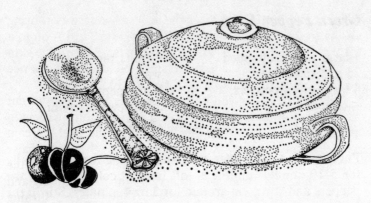

Starters

I've given first courses a chapter to themselves because there are so many to be made in summer. Chilled soups included here are made from tomatoes, avocados, watercress, sorrel and other vegetables. There is even one made from cherries – a Polish soup that is particularly delicious. Although leeks are by no means at the height of their season, you'll find them at the greengrocers; combine them with potatoes to make a delicate vichyssoise. Gazpacho, that Spanish blend of raw peppers, tomatoes, onions and garlic with its garnish of crisp vegetables and croûtons, is almost a meal in itself and, served before a light fish dish, makes a perfect sunshine meal. Bisques made from lobster and crab are here and so are potted shrimps and taramasalata made from smoked cod's roe. I've also included that other favourite found in Greek restaurants – hummus made of pounded chick peas, though more properly it belongs in the Middle East rather than the far end of Europe. Both tomatoes and cucumbers can be made into ices – savoury sorbets with which to begin meals on really hot days – and there are two recipes using salmon: a mousse and brandade for special occasions.

Green Pepper Soup

1 large onion, chopped
25 g (1 oz) butter
4 large green peppers,
   chopped

500 ml (1 pint) boiling
   water
salt and pepper
5 ml (1 level teaspoon)
   caster sugar

Put the onion and butter in a pan and cook the onion gently for 5–10 minutes until it is soft but not coloured. Add the peppers and stir them around for 3 or 4 minutes. Stir in the boiling water and simmer the soup for 40 minutes or until the peppers are really soft. Push this soup through a sieve. If you blend it you'll be left with tiny pieces of pepper skin which spoil the texture. Season it with salt, pepper and caster sugar. Serve hot or cold.

Serves 4–6

Tomato Soup

1 kg (2 lb) ripe tomatoes,
   chopped
salt and pepper
250 ml (½ pint) chicken
   stock

5 ml (1 level teaspoon)
   caster sugar
few sprigs of basil

Put the tomatoes in a large saucepan. Season them with salt and pepper, stir in the stock, sugar and basil and cover the pan. Bring to the boil, then simmer the soup for 20–30 minutes until the tomatoes are very soft. Sieve to remove the skins and seeds and pour the soup back into the pan. Reheat and serve with grated cheese.

Serves 4

Beetroot Soup

1 kg (2 lb) raw beetroot,
grated
1 large onion, finely
chopped

1 litre (1¾ pints) good meat
stock
juice of 1 lemon, strained
salt and pepper
142-g (5-oz) carton soured
cream

Put the beetroot and the onion in a large pan with the stock (beef, chicken, or whatever bones you have boiled with some seasoning – it will give a better flavour than a commercial stock cube). Bring the stock to the boil and simmer the mixture for 30–40 minutes. Turn off the heat and allow to stand for 15 minutes, then strain and add the lemon juice. Add the seasoning and either chill the soup or reheat it gently. Serve with soured cream, whirling it into each plate after lightly beating it in the carton to make it smooth.

Serves 6

Cold Sorrel Soup

225 g (8 oz) sorrel leaves
1 large egg, beaten
1 clove garlic, crushed
2 hard-boiled eggs,
chopped
juice of 1 lemon, strained

salt and pepper
125 ml (¼ pint) double
cream
2·5-cm (1-in) piece
cucumber, thinly sliced

Wash the sorrel leaves and trim off the stems. Chop the leaves coarsely. Put them in a pan with 1 litre (2 pints) cold water, bring to the boil, then simmer for 10 minutes. Allow to cool slightly, then liquidise to a purée. Beat the egg with the garlic and hard-boiled eggs, adding the lemon juice and salt and pepper. Stir this into the sorrel mixture.

Allow to cool completely. Just before serving, stir in the cream and garnish with the cucumber slices.

Serves 4

Vichyssoise

6 large leeks, prepared
2 large potatoes, prepared
1 large onion, sliced
50 g (2 oz) butter
salt and pepper

1 litre (2 pints) chicken stock
125 ml ($\frac{1}{4}$ pint) single cream
15 ml (1 level tablespoon) chives, finely chopped

Discard all but the white parts of the leeks for a classic soup, but you can use the green leaves as well when it's just family. Cut the leeks into 2·5-cm (1-in) pieces. Thinly slice the potatoes. Put the leeks and onion with the butter in a large pan. Fry them gently together for 5 minutes until soft but not coloured. Add the potatoes and salt and pepper, then stir in the stock. Bring to the boil, cover pan and simmer for 40 minutes. Blend the soup or push it through a nylon sieve, stir in the cream and chill it for 2 hours in the fridge. Serve sprinkled with chopped chives.

Serves 4

Cherry Soup

0·75 kg (1$\frac{1}{2}$ lb) cherries, stoned
1 small lemon
5-cm (2-in) cinnamon stick

100 g (4 oz) caster sugar
125 ml ($\frac{1}{4}$ pint) hot water
30 ml (2 tablespoons) port

Morello cherries are best for this soup, but they are not as readily available as sweet ones. If you use the sweet variety, you might find you want to add less sugar. Sweet cherries need a shorter cooking time, too.

Rinse the cherries and put them in a pan with 500 ml (1 pint) cold water. Thinly pare off the lemon rind and add to the cherries with the cinnamon stick. Bring to the boil and cook for 20 minutes until soft. Put the sugar in a pan with the hot water and heat gently to dissolve the sugar. Then bring to the boil and simmer until the mixture is syrupy. Pour on the hot cherries and allow to cool, then chill them in the fridge for 2 hours. Remove the lemon rind and cinnamon. Squeeze out and strain the lemon juice. Taste the soup first then stir in some lemon juice and the port. You may find you need all the lemon juice for your taste.

Serves 4

Cold Cucumber Soup

2 medium-sized cucumbers, peeled
5 ml (1 level teaspoon) onion, finely chopped
25 g (1 oz) butter
25 g (1 oz) plain flour
750 ml (1½ pints) chicken stock
salt and pepper
60 ml (4 tablespoons) single cream
15 ml (1 level tablespoon) mint, finely chopped

Cut 12 slices of cucumber for garnish then cut the remainder into 1·25-cm (½-in) pieces. Fry with the onion in the butter in a large pan, then stir in the flour and cook the mixture for 1 minute without letting it colour. Gradually stir in the stock and bring the soup to the boil, then simmer it for 20 minutes. Blend the soup or push it through a nylon sieve and season it with salt and pepper. Stir in the cream and chill the soup for 2 hours. Pour into individual bowls and lay 3 slices of cucumber on each bowl. Sprinkle with the chopped mint.

Serves 4

Chilled Watercress Soup

2 bunches of watercress,
  prepared
1 small onion, sliced
350 g ($\frac{3}{4}$ lb) potatoes, sliced
50 g (2 oz) butter
500 ml (1 pint) chicken
  stock

250 ml ($\frac{1}{2}$ pint) milk
salt and pepper
1 blade of mace
125 ml ($\frac{1}{4}$ pint) single
  cream

When you prepare the watercress, save a few of the nicest leaves for garnish. Fry the onion and potato slices gently in the butter for about 5 minutes, without allowing the vegetables to colour. Pour in the stock and milk and season with salt and pepper and the blade of mace. Simmer, covered, for about 15 minutes or until the potatoes are almost cooked, then add the watercress and simmer for another 10 minutes. Remove the mace and either blend the soup or push it through a nylon sieve. Allow the soup to cool, then chill it in the fridge for an hour or two. Just before serving, stir in the cream to make a swirl pattern and garnish with the reserved watercress.

Serves 6

Iced Avocado Soup

15 g ($\frac{1}{2}$ oz) butter
5 ml (1 level teaspoon)
  onion, finely chopped
5 ml (1 level teaspoon)
  plain flour
1 chicken stock cube
250 ml ($\frac{1}{2}$ pint) boiling
  water

1 large avocado
15 ml (1 tablespoon) lemon
  juice, strained
250 ml ($\frac{1}{2}$ pint) milk
60 ml (4 tablespoons)
  double cream
salt and pepper
sprigs of dill or fennel

Melt the butter in a pan and fry the onion very gently for 5
minutes but do not let it brown. Stir in the flour and cook,
again gently, for 2 minutes. Dissolve the stock cube in the
boiling water; if you have chicken stock made from bones
use this instead, as it gives a finer flavour. Add the stock
gradually to the pan, stirring all the time. Bring to the boil.

Cut the avocado in half using a stainless steel knife.
Remove the stone and skin and mash the flesh with the
lemon juice to a smooth paste. Stir in half the milk, then
stir in the hot chicken stock to make a smooth mixture. Stir
in the rest of the milk and the cream. Season to taste with
salt and pepper and leave to chill for 2 hours. Don't leave
it overnight because you'll find your lovely soup has discoloured. Pour into bowls and garnish with a sprig or two of
a feathery herb – dill or fennel.

Serves 4

Gazpacho

0·5 kg (1 lb) tomatoes,
  skinned
1 medium-sized onion,
  roughly chopped
1 small green pepper, diced
1 clove garlic, crushed
30 ml (2 tablespoons)
  vinegar

60 ml (4 tablespoons) olive
  oil
salt and pepper
375 ml (¾ pint) tomato
  juice
juice of 1 lemon, strained
croûtons (see page 34)

Cut one of the tomatoes in half, remove the seeds and save
the flesh for garnish. (If the tomatoes are small, reserve
two whole ones.) Add the seeds to the other tomatoes and
chop them roughly. Reserve half the onion and green pepper
for garnish. Put the vegetables for the soup with the garlic,
vinegar, olive oil, salt and pepper, tomato and lemon
juices in an electric blender and blend for 5-10 seconds. This
soup is best if it isn't completely smooth. Chill for at least

1 hour. Meanwhile, dice the reserved tomato flesh and put it in one of four individual bowls. Put the reserved onion and green pepper in two more bowls and the croûtons in the fourth. Pour the soup into a large serving dish and hand round the garnishes separately.

Serves 4

Lobster Bisque

1 large carrot, chopped	6 peppercorns
1 small onion, chopped	few parsley stalks
75 g (3 oz) butter	100 g (4 oz) long-grain rice
1·75 litres (3 pints) fish stock	salt and pepper
1 lobster shell, cooked	Cayenne pepper
225 g (8 oz) lobster meat	125 ml (¼ pint) single cream
1 sprig of thyme	75 ml (5 tablespoons) brandy
1 small bay leaf	

Put the carrot and onion with the butter in a large saucepan and simmer them gently until they turn golden. Pour in the fish stock reserved from cooking the lobster or other fish, or, if you have none, use cold water. Smash the lobster shell with a hammer and add it to the pan with the lobster meat, thyme, bay leaf, peppercorns, parsley stalks, rice and a good pinch of salt. Bring to the boil and simmer for 20 minutes. Remove the lobster shell, the herbs and peppercorns and blend the rest (reserving a few nice pieces of lobster meat to use as a garnish). Sieve to make sure no tiny pieces of shell remain, then reheat the bisque and check the seasoning, adding more salt if necessary. Add pepper and Cayenne and stir in the cream and brandy. Garnish with the reserved pieces of lobster, cut into small chunks, and serve very hot.

A classic bisque should be made with a whole small lobster; although this recipe produces a soup with a little less of a lobster flavour, it is economical because you make use of pieces usually thrown away. Make sure you reserve a few good chunks of white meat when you are dressing a lobster so you can make a delicious bisque for next day using this method. If you do wish to use a whole lobster, this recipe will work but you should cut the amount of rice by half.

Serves 6–8

Crab Bisque

1 small whole crab, cooked (see page 60)	1 blade of mace
1 large carrot, chopped	salt
50 g (2 oz) butter	60 ml (4 tablespoons) double cream
3 litres (5 pints) fish stock	30 ml (2 tablespoons) tomato paste
few parsley stalks	60 ml (4 tablespoons) sherry
6 peppercorns	
2 sprigs of thyme	

Remove the large claws from the crab, then twist off the smaller claws. Remove the crab's undershell by pushing with both thumbs under the wider part. From the crab, remove and throw away the small stomach sac, any green bits and pieces, and the dead men's fingers, which are the lungs. Everything else is edible. Using a teaspoon, scoop the meat from under the shell. Cut the body of the crab in two and, using a skewer, remove the meat. Crack the large claws and remove the meat from them.

Put the carrot with the butter in a large pan and cook it for 10 minutes until it is golden. Pour in the fish stock and add the parsley stalks, peppercorns, thyme, mace and a good pinch of salt. Add the crab shells and the small legs and simmer the mixture for 30 minutes. Remove the shells from the pan together with the parsley, peppercorns, thyme and mace and blend the remainder with the brown and white crab meats, saving some white meat for garnish if you like. Sieve to make sure there are no pieces of shell in the bisque and reheat it gently. Stir in the cream and tomato paste and lastly the sherry. Check the seasoning, adding more salt and pepper if required and stir in any white meat garnish. Serve hot.

Serves 8

Avocado Vinaigrette

2 large avocados   vinaigrette (see page 16)

Using a stainless steel knife, cut the avocados in half lengthwise and prise out the stones. Strain the vinaigrette and cover the avocados immediately with it to prevent the cut surfaces from browning.

Serves 4

Tomato Ice

1 kg (2 lb) ripe tomatoes, chopped
½ small onion, chopped
10 ml (1 dessertspoon) tomato paste

few drops Worcestershire sauce
1 medium-sized lemon
5 ml (1 level teaspoon) caster sugar
few sprigs of mint

Put the tomatoes and onion into a large saucepan, cover, and cook for 25 minutes or until the tomatoes are very soft. Push the mixture through a sieve. Stir in the tomato paste and Worcestershire sauce. Finely grate the rind from the lemon and squeeze out and strain the juice. Add the lemon rind and juice to the tomatoes with the sugar. Pour into ice-cube trays or into a plastic box and freeze in the ice-making compartment of your fridge or in a freezer. Turn out by dipping the base of the tray or box in hot water for a second or two. Tip the ice on to a wooden board, crush with a rolling pin, spoon quickly into glass dishes and serve garnished with mint sprigs.

Serves 6

Potted Shrimps

150 g (6 oz) butter, melted
ground mace
pepper

5 ml (1 teaspoon) lemon
juice, strained
225 g (8 oz) peeled
shrimps

Mix 100 g (4 oz) of the melted butter with ground mace, pepper, lemon juice and the shrimps. Taste for seasoning, adding more if necessary. Pack the mixture into six small serving pots and smooth the tops. Cool them in the fridge until set, then pour on the remaining melted butter and leave to set again. Serve with thin slices of toast.

Serves 6

Taramasalata

225 g (8 oz) smoked cod's
roe, skinned
1 clove garlic, crushed
5 ml (1 level teaspoon)
grated onion

1 large lemon
180 ml (12 tablespoons)
salad oil
pepper

Mash the cod's roe with the garlic and onion. Finely grate the rind from the lemon and squeeze out and strain the juice. Add rind and juice to the cod's roe and pour on half the oil. Leave to stand for 30 minutes then blend the mixture until smooth, gradually adding the remaining oil through the hole in the top of the blender cap. Season with freshly ground white pepper. Taste for seasoning, adding more if necessary. Serve with the flat Greek bread called pitta.

If you find this recipe a little too rich, add about 50 g (2 oz) fresh white breadcrumbs and put in a little less oil.

Serves 4

Avocado Savoury Mousse

2 soft avocados, mashed
1 large lemon
125 ml ($\frac{1}{4}$ pint) single
  cream

15 g ($\frac{1}{2}$ oz) powdered
  gelatine
salt and pepper

Mash the avocados in a large bowl. Finely grate the lemon rind, squeeze out and strain the juice and add immediately to the avocados to prevent them turning brown. Stir in the cream. Dissolve the gelatine in 60 ml (4 tablespoons) cold water in a basin over a saucepan of simmering water. When it is clear, stir in 185 ml ($\frac{1}{4}$ pint plus 4 tablespoons) warm water. Pour this into the avocados, whisking all the time. Season with a little salt and pepper, turn the mixture into a mould and allow to set in the kitchen, not the fridge. This will take about 2 hours. Unmould by dipping it in hot water for a couple of seconds, then turn it on to a serving plate. Serve with a green salad.

Serves 4–6

Brandade de Saumon

0·75 kg (1$\frac{1}{2}$ lb) salmon or
  salmon trout
1 clove garlic, crushed
90 ml (6 tablespoons)
  double cream

125 ml ($\frac{1}{4}$ pint) olive oil
30 ml (2 tablespoons)
  lemon juice, strained
salt and pepper
croûtons (see page 34)

Rinse the fish and put it in a pan. Just cover it with cold water or fish stock made by boiling the bones and other bits and pieces for 10 minutes. Bring slowly to the boil and poach the fish until it is tender, then remove it from the liquid. Flake the fish, removing all skin and bones.

Put the salmon pieces in batches in a blender with the crushed garlic, double cream and oil, blending it all together until it is creamy and smooth. Transfer the mixture to the top of a double saucepan or into a bowl standing over a pan of simmering water. Simmer gently until hot, stirring in the lemon juice, salt and freshly ground white pepper to taste.

Make the croûtons as described on page 34, but instead of cutting them into cubes, cut the bread into triangles using thin slices of bread. Garnish the brandade with the croûtons and serve hot or cold.

Serves 4

Salmon Mousse

0·5 kg (1 lb) salmon or salmon trout pieces, cooked
25 g (1 oz) butter
25 g (1 oz) plain flour
250 ml (½ pint) fish stock from the salmon
2 large eggs, separated
125 ml (¼ pint) double cream, whipped

15 ml (1 tablespoon) lemon juice, strained
30 ml (2 tablespoons) tomato paste
15 g (½ oz) powdered gelatine
45 ml (3 tablespoons) warm water
cucumber slices for garnish

This is an ideal recipe for any small pieces of salmon left over or cut off before preparing another dish. If you have less than 0·5 kg (1 lb) you can simply adjust the quantities of the other ingredients.

Mash the salmon pieces well. Melt the butter in a pan and

stir in the flour. Cook for 1 minute, then remove from the heat and gradually stir in the fish stock. Bring to the boil and simmer for 2 minutes. Beat in the egg yolks and allow the sauce to cool before beating in the cream, lemon juice and tomato paste. Stir in the fish.

Dissolve the gelatine in the warm water in a basin over a pan of simmering water. Whisk it into the salmon mixture. Whisk the egg whites until stiff but not dry, then fold them into the salmon. Pour into a large soufflé dish or into individual ones and leave in a cool place to set. Garnish with the cucumber slices and serve with hot toast.

Serves 6–8

Hummus

225 g (½ lb) chick peas
salt
1 clove garlic, crushed
125 ml (¼ pint) tahini
105 ml (7 tablespoons)
  lemon juice, strained

15 ml (1 tablespoon)
  sesame oil
15 ml (1 level tablespoon)
  parsley, finely chopped

Soak the chick peas in plenty of cold water overnight. Next day, drain them and cover them with fresh cold water in a pan and bring them to the boil. Simmer for 2 hours or until they are soft, adding more water from time to time whenever necessary. When they are soft, drain them and keep the cooking liquid. Pound the chick peas to a smooth paste with a pestle and mortar or push them through a fine vegetable mill. Season with a good pinch of salt and stir in the garlic. Add some of the cooking liquid at this stage to thin the purée to a thick cream. Gradually beat in the tahini and lemon juice alternately and when these are incorporated taste for seasoning, adding more if necessary. Pour the hummus on to a flat plate and pour a thin film of sesame oil over the top. Sprinkle with the parsley and serve with pitta, the flat Greek bread.

Tahini is a sesame seed paste which can be bought from Cypriot or Middle Eastern shops.

Serves 4–6

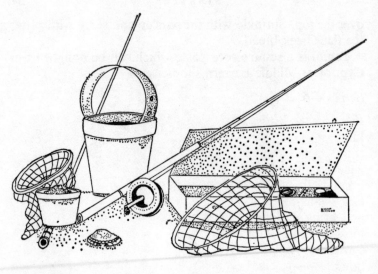

Fish

Trout, salmon trout and the king of the freshwater fish, the salmon, make their appearance during June, July and August. Add to this the lobster and crab and pickings are rich at the fishmonger's – if you are rich. Even halibut and red mullet are pricey these days. So although I've given all the classic ways of preparing these various fish, I've also included lots of lovely recipes using small pieces.

Of course, if you know any keen fisherman, you really score and can prepare blue trout, which is only possible with freshly caught and killed fish. Dover sole and plaice also are at their best during the summer months and plaice makes a very good substitute in many dishes for the more expensive sole. Goujons, for instance, small strips of flat white fish coated in egg and breadcrumbs and deep fried, can be made economically of plaice, because in the end you don't taste much of the fish, particularly if you serve the traditional sauce – a spicy tartare.

Dressed Lobster

0·5–0·75 kg (1¼–1½ lb) lobster   1 large lemon, sliced
oil   watercress, prepared
mayonnaise (see page 40)

If you have a live lobster there are two humane ways of killing it. One is to push a very sharp pointed knife down through the shell at the centre of the cross at the back of the head, holding the lobster firmly with your other hand. The other is to put the lobster into a large pan of salt water (sea water preferably, or plain water and coarse sea salt) and bring it slowly to the boil. At about 20°C (70°F) the lobster faints and dies almost immediately. Tests have shown that this is preferable to plunging the lobster into boiling water. The first method should be used if you want to grill the lobster and then serve it simply with lemon wedges and melted butter. Use the second method for this recipe.

Once the water has come to the boil, simmer gently, allowing about 25 minutes for this weight of lobster. Lift the lobster from the water and allow to cool, rubbing the shell with a little oil before splitting it. Twist off the claws. Using a very sharp knife, split the lobster down the centre back into two halves. Remove the dark intestine which runs all the way along the lobster and remove the stomach sac and the gills. The liver is a delicacy, and though a green colour, should not be discarded. Keep, too, the bright red spawn or coral found under the tail of female lobsters.

Using a skewer, pick out the meat from the tail, cut it into chunks and return it to the shell. Crack the claws using a small hammer and remove the meat. There's good meat in the small claws which shouldn't be wasted, although it's more fiddly to get out. Put all the meat, finely chopped, back into the body shell. Arrange the half shells on two plates. Spread a little of the mayonnaise over the surface of the meat in the shells and decorate it with the coral, if you've bought a female lobster. Serve with the rest of the mayonnaise in a bowl and garnish the plates with lemon slices and some watercress.

Serves 2

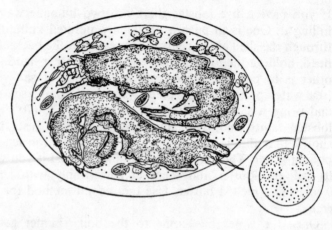

Dressed Crab

1 kg (2 lb) crab, cooked
salt
5 ml (1 teaspoon) cooking
   oil
15 ml (1 tablespoon) lemon
   juice, strained
30 ml (2 tablespoons)
   double cream

pepper
mayonnaise (see page 40)
2 hard-boiled eggs
30 ml (2 level tablespoons)
   parsley, finely chopped
lettuce leaves, prepared

You can buy a boiled crab but make sure the one you choose has both claws intact. If you are going to cook a crab put it in cold salted water (again sea water is best) and bring it slowly to the boil, then simmer it for 20 minutes. Allow to cool in the liquid, then remove and drain. Twist off the large claws, then twist off the small claws. Remove the undershell by pushing it up with both thumbs under the wider part. From the crab, remove and throw away the small stomach sac, any green bits and pieces and the dead men's fingers which are the lungs. Using a teaspoon, take out the brown meat from the shell and put it in a bowl.

Hold the main shell firmly, and using a knife handle, break the shell along the line. Wash the shell, dry it and rub it with a little oil to make it shine. Cut the body of the crab in two and remove all the white meat with a skewer and put it in another bowl, separate from the brown meat. Crack the large claws using a small hammer and remove the white meat and add it to the bowl.

Mix the brown meat with 10 ml (2 teaspoons) lemon juice, the cream and plenty of freshly ground black pepper. Mix the white meat with salt and pepper and the rest of the lemon juice.

Arrange the white meat in the shell at each side and spoon the brown meat in the centre. Coat with a little of the mayonnaise. Separate the yolks from the hard-boiled whites and sieve them. Finely chop the whites. Decorate the mayonnaise with fine lines of egg yolk, egg white and parsley and arrange the crab on a bed of lettuce leaves. Garnish with the small claws (shined with a little oil) and serve the rest of the mayonnaise in a bowl.

Serves 4

Blue Trout

4 small trout	1 small carrot, sliced
60 ml (4 tablespoons) vinegar	1 small onion, chopped
100 g (4 oz) unsalted butter	few parsley stalks
	1 bay leaf
Court bouillon:	6 peppercorns
1 litre (1¾ pints) dry white wine mixed with water	10 ml (2 level teaspoons) salt
	15 ml (1 tablespoon) lemon juice, strained

This recipe only works with freshly-caught and killed river trout, so if your husband's a keen fisherman, try out this method of cooking his catch.

Clean the trout, leaving on the heads and tails. Rinse them and put them in a large saucepan, or two. Add the vinegar. Put all the ingredients for the court bouillon in a large pan. Bring to the boil and simmer for 30 minutes. Strain and add to the fish while still boiling. Watch the fish curl round, then reduce the heat and simmer them for 15 minutes or until tender. Lift the fish from the court bouillon, drain well and arrange on serving plates. Melt the butter in a small pan and pour it over the fish to serve.

Serves 4

Trout with Almonds

4 small trout	150 g (6 oz) unsalted butter
salt and pepper	50 g (2 oz) flaked almonds
plain flour	1 large lemon

Ask your fishmonger to clean the trout but to leave the heads and tails on. Wipe them well. Season some plain flour and use to dust the trout. Melt 50 g (2 oz) butter in a large frying pan and fry two trout for about 10 minutes or until golden brown on both sides. Use another 50 g (2 oz) butter for the remaining trout. Remove from the pan and keep them hot on serving plates. Melt the remaining butter in another small frying pan, add the almonds and heat gently until they are golden brown, turning them all the time. Cut the lemon in half and squeeze out and strain the juice from one half. When the butter is slightly brown too, pour in the lemon juice and pour the butter and almonds over the trout. Cut the remaining lemon half into wedges and use to garnish the fish.

Serves 4

Glazed Salmon

1 salmon or salmon trout
court bouillon (see page
   61)
500 ml (1 pint) packet
   aspic

radishes, cucumber, olives
   and dill or fennel for
   garnish
mayonnaise (see page 40)

Ask your fishmonger to clean the fish but to leave it whole
with the head and tail intact. Arrange it on a large piece of
foil and lower it on the foil into your largest saucepan. You
might need to curl it a little. Keep the foil round the fish
to help when lifting it out. Pour on the boiling, strained court
bouillon and poach the fish for 10 minutes per 0·5 kg (1 lb)
for the first 2 kg (5 lb) then 5 minutes per 0·5 kg (1 lb) for
the next 2 kg (5 lb). Allow the fish to cool to lukewarm in the
cooking liquid, then lift it carefully with the aid of the foil on
to a wire cake rack. Rip the foil at one end of the fish and
continue tearing it, holding it flat, until it tears from under
the fish without disturbing it. Remove the skin.

Now's the time to remove the backbone for really easy
carving. Carefully loosen the flesh near the head and tail
at the backbone. Do this slightly underneath the backbone,
rather than on top, which is the side you'll see. Using scissors
snip through the bone at both ends and gently ease and pull
it out. Neaten the flesh again, smoothing it with a round-
bladed knife.

Make up the aspic according to the directions on the
packet. Allow it to cool to lukewarm, then spoon a thin coat
over the complete fish and let it set. Cut the radishes into
thin slices, cut thin pieces of cucumber skin into the shapes
of leaves and stems, and cut thin slices of cucumber and
olive, preferably the stuffed variety. If the aspic in the bowl
has set, keep it liquid by stirring it over a pan of hot water.
Using a hat pin, dip each piece of decoration in liquid aspic
and place it on the fish. Let all the decorations set, then spoon
another coat of liquid aspic over the fish and let it set.

Transfer very gently on to a serving dish and chop the remaining jelly using a wet knife and use to garnish all round the fish. Serve with the mayonnaise.

Serves 6–8

Salmon with Hollandaise Sauce

4 salmon steaks, about 1·75 cm (¾ in) thick	15 ml (1 tablespoon) warm water
court bouillon (see page 61)	150 g (6 oz) unsalted butter, softened
	salt and pepper
Hollandaise sauce:	15 ml (1 tablespoon) lemon
3 large egg yolks	juice, strained

Wipe the salmon steaks, tuck in the flaps of skin and secure them in a good shape with cocktail sticks. Arrange them in a frying pan or a shallow baking but flameproof dish. Pour on the cold court bouillon and bring slowly to the boil. Cover the pan or dish and simmer the fish for 5 to 10 minutes or until no longer translucent. You can test with a skewer by pushing it into the thickest flesh. You'll feel no resistance if the fish is cooked, but it's difficult to do this without marking it.

While the fish simmers, make the hollandaise sauce. Whisk the egg yolks with the warm water in a large basin standing over a pan of gently simmering water. Make sure the base of the bowl is well above the water and keep the heat low. Use a hand electric whisk and very gradually whisk in small dabs of the butter. When half the butter is incorporated, the danger time for this sauce is past and you can add the remaining butter a little more quickly. Season with a little salt and plenty of white pepper and add the lemon juice.

Remove the cocktail sticks from the fish as you put it on serving plates and spoon the sauce to cover half the fish including the skin flaps. If you wish to remove the skins before serving, use a fork rather like a sardine can opener. With the fork upright, catch one end of the skin between two tines of the fork and turn the fork round to secure the end. Continue rolling the fork and the skin will roll round it and off the salmon steak.

Serves 4

Coulibiac

Rich pastry:
450 g (1 lb) plain flour
pinch of salt
225 g (8 oz) unsalted butter
75 g (3 oz) lard
iced water

Salmon filling:
court bouillon (see page 61)
1 kg (2 lb) salmon pieces
100 g (4 oz) unsalted butter
225 g (8 oz) button mushrooms, thinly sliced

30 ml (2 tablespoons) lemon juice, strained
salt and pepper
225 g ($\frac{1}{2}$ lb) onions, finely chopped
50 g (2 oz) long-grain rice
125 ml ($\frac{1}{4}$ pint) fish stock
3 hard-boiled eggs, chopped
15 ml (1 level tablespoon) dill, chopped
1 large egg, beaten

Sift the flour and salt into a bowl. Cut the butter and lard into small pieces and, working quickly, rub it in. Add 120 ml (8 tablespoons) iced water and mix to a dough adding another 15 or 30 ml (1 or 2 tablespoons) iced water if the dough seems crumbly. Divide the pastry in half, wrap each half in greaseproof paper and chill in the fridge for 2 hours until firm.

Bring the court bouillon to the boil in a pan and lower in the rinsed fish pieces. You can use off-cuts for this dish because the fish will be flaked. Simmer for 5 minutes, transfer the fish to a large plate, remove the skin and bones and separate the fish into large flakes. Reserve the cooking liquid.

Melt 25 g (1 oz) butter in a large pan and cook the mushrooms for 3 minutes until soft, stirring all the time. Stir in the lemon juice and salt and pepper to taste. Transfer to another plate. Melt 50 g (2 oz) butter in another pan and fry the onions for 5 minutes until golden and soft. Season and transfer to a third plate. Melt the remaining butter in the pan, add the rice and fry it for 1 minute, then pour on 125 ml ($\frac{1}{4}$ pint) reserved fish stock and simmer the rice for 15 minutes until the rice is moist and cooked and the liquid has been absorbed.

Roll out one piece of the pastry to a large, very thin rectangle, about 25 cm by 35 cm (10 in by 14 in). Transfer it to a large greased baking tray. Roll the other piece of pastry to a similar size. Arrange the fish in one layer topped with the onion, then the mushrooms, then the rice and finally the eggs and sprinkle with the herbs. Brush the pastry round the filling with a little of the beaten egg mixed with 15 ml (1 tablespoon) cold water. Put the second piece of pastry on top and press the edges to seal. Trim the edges and decorate them. Use any pastry trimmings to decorate the top of the coulibiac, sticking them in place with beaten egg. Brush the whole thing with egg and bake it at 200°C (400°F)/Gas 6 for about 1 hour or until golden brown. Serve cut into thick slices with a dish of soured cream.

Serves 8

Salmon Tourte

Shortcrust pastry:
225 g (8 oz) plain flour
pinch of salt
50 g (2 oz) margarine
50 g (2 oz) lard

Salmon filling:
325 g (¾ lb) raw salmon,
   thinly sliced
100 g (4 oz) button
   mushrooms, chopped
50 g (2 oz) unsalted butter
125 ml (¼ pint) single
   cream
60 ml (4 tablespoons) dry
   white wine

salt and pepper
ground nutmeg
2 large egg whites, whisked

Lemon butter:
25 g (1 oz) unsalted butter
30 ml (2 tablespoons)
   lemon juice, strained
5 ml (1 level teaspoon)
   chives, snipped
5 ml (1 level teaspoon)
   lemon thyme, chopped
5 ml (1 level teaspoon)
   parsley, finely chopped
salt and pepper

Sift the flour and salt into a bowl for the pastry. Rub in the margarine and lard and mix to a stiff dough with cold water. Divide the pastry in two halves and roll one half to line a 20-cm (8-in) flan ring. Roll the rest of the pastry to form a top for the flan.

Reserve some of the best slices of salmon to form a thin layer in the pie and mash or blend the rest with the mushrooms, butter, cream and wine to a smooth paste. Season with salt and pepper and ground nutmeg. Fold in the whisked egg whites. Put half this mixture into the flan case and smooth the top. Cover with a layer of the reserved salmon slices, then spread the remaining salmon cream over the top. Cover with the round of shortcrust pastry, seal the edges, and trim and decorate them. Make a hole in the centre of the top crust and decorate the tourte with any left-over pieces of pastry. Bake at 200°C (400°F)/Gas 6 for 30 to 35 minutes or until the pastry is golden brown.

To make the lemon butter, melt the butter and whisk in the lemon juice, chives, thyme and parsley and a little salt and pepper. Pour this through the hole in the top crust and serve at once.

Serves 6–8

Sole Véronique

8 lemon sole fillets	*Velouté sauce:*
½ small onion, finely chopped	15 g (½ oz) butter
few parsley stalks	15 g (½ oz) plain flour
1 small bay leaf	250 ml (½ pint) fish stock
salt and pepper	100 g (4 oz) white seedless grapes
60 ml (4 tablespoons) dry white wine	salt and pepper
	45 ml (3 tablespoons) single cream

Rinse the fish fillets and arrange them in a shallow oven-proof dish. Add the onion, parsley stalks, bay leaf and salt and pepper. Pour on the wine and 125 ml (¼ pint) cold water. Cover the dish with foil and bake it at 180°C (350°F)/Gas 4 for 10–15 minutes. Lift the fish on to a serving dish and keep hot. Measure 250 ml (½ pint) of the strained fish liquid for the sauce.

Melt the butter in a pan, stir in the flour and cook the mixture for 1 minute. Remove from the heat and gradually stir in the stock. Bring to the boil, stirring all the time, then cook the sauce for 2 minutes. Meanwhile peel the grapes, keeping them whole. (If you are using grapes *with* seeds, remove them at this stage by halving the grapes.) Season the sauce with salt and pepper and stir in the cream. Stir in most of the grapes and pour the sauce over the fish. Garnish with reserved grapes.

Serves 4

Sole Cushions

0·5 kg (1 lb) lemon sole
  fillets
125 ml (¼ pint) béchamel
  sauce (see page 30)
50 g (2 oz) peas, cooked

5 ml (1 level teaspoon)
  lemon thyme, chopped
15 ml (1 tablespoon)
  double cream
369-g (13-oz) packet frozen
  puff pastry

Rinse the fish fillets and put them in a pan. Just cover with
cold water, bring them to the boil and simmer for 10 minutes.
When cool enough to handle, remove the dark skin and
flake the fish. Mix with the béchamel sauce and the peas
and stir in the thyme and cream. Roll the pastry on a lightly-
floured board to a 30-cm (12-in) square and cut it into 4
smaller squares. Spoon a quarter of the filling in the centre
of each square. Moisten the edges with cold water and bring
all four points to the centre like an envelope. Press to seal,
then crimp them into a pattern. Arrange them on baking
sheets and bake them at 220°C (425°F)/Gas 7 for about 40
minutes until golden brown and puffy.

Serves 4

Dover Sole Meunière

4 small Dover sole
salt and pepper
plain flour
125 g (5 oz) unsalted butter

30 ml (2 level tablespoons)
  parsley, chopped
30 ml (2 tablespoons)
  lemon juice, strained
1 large lemon, sliced

Rinse the fish and cut off the fins. Make a small cut through
the skin just above the tail and with your fingers loosen the
skin from the tail and around the edges. Dip your fingers in
salt, grip the skin and rip it off towards the head. You can
remove the white skin in the same way but unless the fish

are really large, this is usually left on. Add salt and pepper to some flour and dust each fish with this.

Melt 25 g (1 oz) butter in each of two large frying pans and fry one fish in each pan, skinned side first, for about 5 minutes, then turn them and fry the other side until it too is golden brown. Remove on to serving plates and keep hot while you fry the remaining fish using another 25 g (1 oz) butter for each one.

Wipe out one of the pans and melt the remaining butter in it. Heat gently until it turns golden brown, then add the parsley and lemon juice and pour immediately over the fish. Garnish with lemon slices and serve at once.

Serves 4

Goujons

8 sole or plaice fillets	*Crisp sauce:*
salt and pepper	mayonnaise (see page 40)
50 g (2 oz) plain flour	30 ml (2 level tablespoons)
1 large egg, beaten	celery, chopped
225 g (8 oz) fresh white	30 ml (2 level tablespoons)
breadcrumbs	cucumber, chopped
oil for deep frying	30 ml (2 tablespoons)
	soured cream
	paprika

Rinse the fish and skin the fillets (see page 69 for instructions for sole). If you are using plaice, put the fillets skin side down on a wooden board and, using a very sharp small knife, saw the flesh away from the skin at the tail end. Dip your fingers in salt to give a good grip on the end of the skin and continue sawing the flesh from the skin, keeping the knife blade flat against the skin. Cut each fillet into ribbons about 10 cm long and 1·25 cm wide (4 × ½ in). Mix a good pinch of salt and pepper with the flour and toss in the fish to coat. Shake off excess, then dip the fillets first in egg and then breadcrumbs, patting them on well and then shaking off the excess. Heat the oil to 193°C (380°F) and fry the fish in batches for about 5 minutes or until golden brown. Drain well on kitchen paper.

Stir the mayonnaise with the celery and cucumber and mix in the soured cream. Season with paprika and serve with the goujons.

Serves 4

Fried Plaice

4 plaice fillets, skinned
plain flour
salt and pepper
1 large egg, beaten
100 g (4 oz) fresh white
   breadcrumbs
75 g (3 oz) unsalted butter

Tartare sauce:
125 ml (¼ pint) mayonnaise
   (see page 40)
5 ml (1 teaspoon) dry
   white wine or white
   vinegar

5 ml (1 teaspoon) Dijon
   mustard
1 medium-sized onion,
   finely grated
2 large gherkins, finely
   chopped
salt and pepper
15 ml (1 level tablespoon)
   parsley, chopped
5 ml (1 level teaspoon)
   tarragon, chopped

Rinse the fish and dry on kitchen paper. Season some flour with salt and pepper and use to dust each fillet. Dip each one in beaten egg and then in the breadcrumbs, patting them on well then shaking off the excess.

Divide the butter between two large frying pans and fry the fillets, skinned side down, for 3 or 4 minutes until golden brown. Turn them and fry the other side until golden too. Drain on kitchen paper and serve with the tartare sauce made by beating the mayonnaise with the wine or vinegar to thin it a little, then stirring in the rest of the ingredients.

Serves 2

Seafood Timbales

4 large plaice fillets, skinned   250 ml (½ pint) packet
100 g (4 oz) peeled shrimps   aspic
2·5-cm (1-in) piece   salt and pepper
   cucumber   watercress, prepared

Rinse the plaice fillets and shrimps. Cut off the cucumber
skin and trim it into 16 small diamond shapes. Chop the
cucumber into small dice. Make up the aspic according to
the directions on the packet. Allow it to cool, then keep it
from setting by stirring it occasionally over a pan of
simmering water.

Meanwhile, poach the plaice fillets in a little water for 10
minutes until no longer transparent. Pour a little of the
aspic into 8 timbale or dariole moulds. Allow to set. Using
a hat pin, dip each piece of cucumber skin in liquid aspic
and arrange 2 in each mould, skin side down, leaving space
in the middle for a shrimp. Allow to set, then dip and
arrange 8 shrimps in the centres. Allow to set, pour on a
little aspic to cover the shrimps and allow this to set.

Flake the fish and season it with pepper but not too much
salt as the shrimps will be slightly salty. Mix with the remaining shrimps and the chopped cucumber and the rest of the
aspic. Spoon into the moulds and leave to set. To unmould
the timbales, dip them swiftly in very hot water for a couple
of seconds, then turn them out on to a wet hand and slip
them into position on a wet serving plate. If you get one in
the wrong place, it will slip about on the wet surface while
you position it correctly. Surround with the watercress and
serve with a salad.

Serves 4

Grilled Red Mullet

4 small red mullet
45 ml (3 tablespoons) oil
45 ml (3 tablespoons)
  vinegar

1 small onion, chopped
8 peppercorns, crushed
1 bay leaf

Ask your fishmonger to clean the mullet but to leave them whole. Rinse the fish and wipe well. Arrange them in a dish in one layer. Pour on the oil and vinegar and sprinkle with the onion, peppercorns and bay leaf. Leave to marinate for 2 hours, turning the fish frequently.

Drain off the marinade and put the fish on a greased grill pan. Cook under a medium heat for about 7 minutes each side, basting occasionally with the marinade. Serve with a broad bean salad or ratatouille.

Serves 4

Red Mullet in a Parcel

6 red mullet
100 g (4 oz) butter,
  softened
salt and pepper

few sprigs of dill or chervil
1 large lemon
5 ml (1 level teaspoon)
  chives, snipped

Ask your fishmonger to clean the mullet but to leave on the heads and tails. Rinse the fish well and dry them on kitchen paper. Cut a large oval piece of greaseproof paper for each fish and spread each piece in the centre with butter. Lay a fish on each and sprinkle with a little salt and pepper, grinding it from a mill. Add the dill or chervil sprigs. Finely grate the rind from the lemon and squeeze out and strain the juice. Pour the juice over the fish and sprinkle with the lemon rind. Finally add the chives. Fold the paper over the fish (like a pasty) and turn the edges over twice to seal. Pleat the edges to make a tight seal. Arrange the parcels on baking trays and bake the fish at 180°C (350°F)/Gas 4 for about 15 minutes. Test one by pressing it through the paper; when it feels soft the fish are done. Serve each person with a parcel to unwrap themselves.

Serves 6

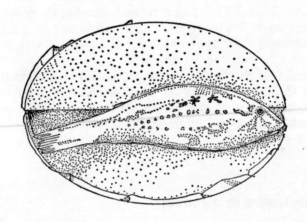

Halibut Mornay

0·75 kg (1½ lb) halibut fillets	velouté sauce (see page 68)
1 large lemon, sliced	75 g (3 oz) Cheddar cheese, grated
few sprigs of parsley	142-g (5-oz) carton single
salt and pepper	cream
1 bay leaf	25 g (1 oz) Parmesan
250 ml (½ pint) milk	cheese, grated

Rinse the fish fillets and lay them in a large ovenproof dish. Cover with the lemon slices and add parsley sprigs, a good pinch each of salt and pepper, the bay leaf and milk. Cover the dish with foil and bake at 180°C (350°F)/Gas 4 for about 20 minutes. Strain off the liquid and use to make the velouté sauce. Stir 50 g (2 oz) grated Cheddar cheese and the cream into the sauce. Remove the skin from the fish and pour over the sauce. Mix the remaining cheeses together, sprinkle over the sauce and grill under a medium grill for about 5 minutes until the top is golden brown and bubbling.

Serves 4

Prawns in Soured Cream

50 g (2 oz) butter
juice of 1 lemon, strained
142-g (5-oz) carton soured
　cream
2 egg yolks
salt and pepper

325 g (12 oz) peeled prawns
4 slices white bread,
　toasted
10 ml (2 level teaspoons)
　chives, snipped

Melt the butter in a pan and stir in the lemon juice, soured cream and egg yolks. Simmer over a very low heat, stirring all the time, until the sauce thickens – but don't let it boil or you'll have a curdled mess. Season it with salt and pepper (not too much salt because the prawns may be salty) and stir in the prawns. Heat slowly for 5 minutes. Cut the crusts off the bread and serve the prawns garnished with toast triangles and sprinkled with chives.

Serves 4

Curried Prawns

1 kg (2 lb) Dublin Bay
   prawns
salt and pepper
Cayenne pepper
5 ml (1 level teaspoon)
   ground turmeric
60 ml (4 tablespoons) white
   vinegar
1 large lemon
5 ml (1 level teaspoon)
   ground cumin
45 ml (3 tablespoons)
   cooking oil
2·5-cm (1-in) piece green
   root ginger, peeled
1 clove garlic, crushed

1 large onion, finely
   chopped
0·5 kg (1 lb) ripe tomatoes,
   skinned
15 ml (1 level tablespoon)
   dark brown sugar
30 ml (2 level tablespoons)
   coriander, chopped
1 hot green chilli, chopped

Saffron rice:
pinch of saffron stamens
750 ml (1½ pints) boiling
   water
325 g (12 oz) long-grain
   rice

Peel the prawns carefully and remove the intestinal vein by slitting the prawn down the back until the dark thread is exposed, then removing it with the point of a knife. Rinse the prawns well and dry them with kitchen paper. Mix 10 ml (2 level teaspoons) salt in a small bowl with a good pinch of black pepper and Cayenne pepper. Add the turmeric and vinegar. Finely grate the rind from the lemon and squeeze out and strain the juice. Add both to the bowl with the cumin and mix well. Pour this marinade over the prawns and leave them for 1 hour, turning them frequently.

Heat the oil in a heavy frying pan. Chop the ginger finely and add it to the pan with the garlic and onion and cook with a good pinch of salt for about 8 minutes until the onions are golden, turning the mixture often.

Chop the tomatoes and drain the marinade from the prawns. Add both to the frying pan and cook the mixture, stirring for 5 minutes, then add the sugar and coriander. Mix in the prawns until well coated, sprinkle with the chilli and heat through for about 5 minutes until the prawns are cooked. Transfer to a large hot dish and serve with a saffron rice made by steeping the saffron in the boiling water for 15 minutes and then straining the liquid and using it to cook the rice.

Serves 4–6

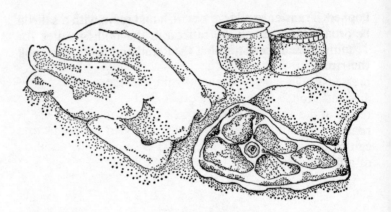

Meat

New lamb in spring, game in autumn and the goose and turkey in winter all have their place in the calendar, but the summer doesn't have any such obvious additions to the butchers' shop windows. Game begins its season in August, with grouse available from the 'glorious twelfth', but taste improves and prices fall in the autumn, so you'll find ideas for using game in the next book. There should be some home-produced veal around but with prices soaring, it's not so evident in the shops as it was even a few years ago. Most of our splendid produce goes abroad. But if you want to make some veal dishes there is a good selection here, including the veal and ham pie which uses pie veal, the cheapest buy of the veal cuts, plus some classic dishes such as Wiener schnitzel and vitello tonnato.

Although a lot of the summer dishes you will want to make will be served cold, there are a few delicious hot dishes using summer vegetables – moussaka (properly made with aubergines), stuffed marrow and stuffed tomatoes. The tomato stuffing, from Turkey, can be used for peppers too.

Peppers require about 5 minutes' blanching in boiling water before stuffing, and will need a longer time in the oven.

Of the cold dishes, I have included those which you might well make for a buffet lunch or a wedding reception – pressed tongue, chicken chaudfroid, cutlets in pastry, vol-au-vents and a galantine. Potted beef – an old country recipe and a very good way of using up a small piece of the roast – suits all occasions from the party to the picnic and can be dressed for the grandest occasions with the addition of a few sprigs of herbs to its butter topping.

Vitello Tonnato

1 kg (2 lb) leg of veal, boned
198-g (7-oz) can tuna in olive oil
2 large carrots, finely chopped
1 large onion, finely chopped
125 ml (¼ pint) dry white wine

6 anchovy fillets, finely chopped
60 ml (4 tablespoons) white wine vinegar
salt and pepper
olive oil
2 hard-boiled egg yolks, mashed
15 ml (1 level tablespoon) capers, finely chopped

Rinse the veal and put it in a large pan with the tuna and its oil, the carrots and onion, wine, anchovy fillets, wine vinegar, 125 ml (¼ pint) cold water and a good pinch each of salt and pepper. Bring slowly to the boil, cover the pan and simmer the meat gently for about 1½ hours or until it is very tender. Remove from the cooking liquid and leave it to cool. Boil the liquid hard to reduce it to about two-thirds of its original quantity.

Push the cooking liquid through a sieve to make a smooth sauce, then stir in enough olive oil to make a flowing sauce. Beat in the egg yolks and the capers. Cut the veal into thin slices and spread each slice with some of the sauce. Arrange the veal in a deep serving dish, cover it with the remaining sauce, cover the dish and leave it in the fridge overnight.

Serves 6–8

Pressed Tongue

2 kg (4 lb) fresh ox tongue	1 bay leaf
1 large carrot, peeled	3 parsley stalks
1 large onion, skinned	1 sprig of thyme
6 peppercorns	1 blade of mace

Rinse the ox tongue, then skewer it into a round shape. Put it in a large saucepan and cover it with cold water. Bring to the boil, then drain. Cover with fresh cold water and add the carrot, onion, peppercorns, bay leaf, parsley stalks, thyme and mace. Bring to the boil, cover, and simmer for 4–5 hours or until the tongue is tender. Skim the cooking liquid from time to time.

Lift the cooked tongue from the pan and plunge it into cold water. As soon as it's cool enough to handle, remove the skin and the small bones and gristle. Curl the tongue into an 18-cm (7-in) cake tin with a fixed base. Continue boiling the cooking liquid until it is reduced to about 250 ml ($\frac{1}{2}$ pint). Strain it over the tongue and place a small plate on top, small enough to go inside the cake tin. Add a weight to the plate and leave the tongue for 4–6 hours to press and set. Turn it out on to a serving plate and garnish with salads.

Serves 8

Veal in Soured Cream

25 g (1 oz) butter
1 kg (2 lb) pie veal, cubed
2 medium-sized onions,
  chopped
250 ml (½ pint) good
  chicken stock
good pinch of salt
5 ml (1 level teaspoon)
  paprika

15 ml (1 tablespoon)
  tomato paste
175 g (6 oz) button
  mushroom caps
142-g (5-oz) carton soured
  cream
5 ml (1 teaspoon) lemon
  juice, strained

Heat the butter in a frying pan and fry the meat for 5 minutes until golden. Add the onion and fry it until golden, too. Pour in the chicken stock, add the salt, paprika and tomato paste and cover and cook the veal for 1 hour or until it is tender. Add the mushrooms, halved if large, to the pan 30 minutes before the end of the cooking time. Just before serving, stir in the soured cream and lemon juice and check the seasoning. Serve with plain boiled rice.

Serves 6

Raised Veal and Ham Pie

Hot water crust pastry:
225 g (8 oz) plain flour
5 ml (1 level teaspoon) salt
50 g (2 oz) lard
60 ml (4 tablespoons) milk

Filling:
325 g (12 oz) pie veal
100 g (4 oz) cooked ham

15 ml (1 level tablespoon)
  parsley, finely chopped
1 large lemon
375 ml (¾ pint) good
  chicken stock
salt and pepper
1 hard-boiled egg, shelled
1 large egg, beaten
10 ml (2 level teaspoons)
  powdered gelatine

Sift the flour and salt into a bowl. Put the lard and milk with 60 ml (4 tablespoons) cold water in a pan. Bring it to the boil and pour it at once into the flour. Mix quickly, using a wooden spoon, until the dough begins to stick together. As soon as it's cool enough to handle knead the dough on a lightly-floured work surface until it is smooth. If it remains at all lumpy add some boiling water, drop by drop, until it is smooth. When the dough is smooth, cut off a third for the lid and keep it warm on a lightly-floured plate standing over a bowl of boiling water. Cover the dough with a tea towel. Work quickly with the large piece because as it cools it becomes hard and difficult to mould.

Flour a 1-kg (2-lb) jam jar and turn it upside down. Mould the larger piece of dough over the bottom and down the sides of the jam jar.

Keep the walls of the dough just less than 1·25-cm ($\frac{1}{2}$-in) thick and the edge fairly straight. Leave it to set for 15 minutes on the jam jar.

Meanwhile, cut the veal and ham into small pieces and mix them with the parsley. Finely grate the rind from the lemon and squeeze out and strain the juice. Add both to the veal mixture and moisten the meat with a little of the stock. Season with salt and pepper. Carefully remove the jam jar from the pastry case and fill the case with the meat mixture and push the hard-boiled egg into the centre. Use the reserved pastry to make a lid for the pie, put it in place and press the edges to seal them. Using scissors, cut round the join to neaten it and then decorate it using your thumb and index finger. Make a hole in the centre of the lid. Tie a deep band of greaseproof paper round the pie and secure it in place with pins. Brush the top of the pie with egg. Bake it at 220°C (425°F)/Gas 7 for 15 minutes, then lower the heat to 180°C (350°F)/Gas 4 and cook the pie for a further hour. Test the meat through the hole and when it's within 30 minutes of being completely cooked, remove the greaseproof paper, brush the whole pie with egg and complete the cooking.

Sprinkle the gelatine on the reserved stock and heat it very gently until the gelatine has dissolved. When the pie comes out of the oven, pour this stock through a funnel into the hole in the top crust and leave it to set before cutting.

Serves 8

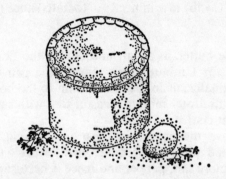

Wiener Schnitzel

4 slices of leg of veal	50 g (2 oz) fresh white
25 g (1 oz) plain flour	breadcrumbs
salt and pepper	100 g (4 oz) unsalted butter
1 large egg, beaten	50 g (2 oz) lard
	1 large lemon, sliced

Ask your butcher to beat the veal until it is very thin. Dust the veal with flour, then coat it first in the seasoned egg and then in the breadcrumbs. Pat the crumbs on well, then shake off the excess. Make sure that the frying pans (you'll need two) are heating with the butter and lard mixture because as soon as the veal has been coated it should be put into the hot fat.

Cook the veal on one side for about 4 minutes, then turn each piece carefully and cook the other side until it too is golden brown. Transfer to kitchen paper to drain and serve immediately with lemon slices.

Serves 4

Veal Loaf

75 g (3 oz) butter	3 large eggs, beaten
75 g (3 oz) plain flour	60 ml (4 tablespoons)
250 ml (½ pint) milk	double cream
salt and pepper	ground mace
0·75 kg (1½ lb) raw minced	tomato sauce (see page 22)
veal	

Melt the butter in a pan and stir in the flour. Cook this mixture for 1 minute, then remove the pan from the heat and gradually stir in the milk. Bring to the boil and simmer the mixture for 1 minute. Season well with salt and pepper, and let it cool.

Remove the paper and beat in the veal, eggs, double cream and plenty of ground mace. Check the seasoning, adding more salt, pepper and mace if necessary. Spoon this mixture into a 15-cm (6-in) soufflé dish and smooth the top. Cover with foil and put it in the top of a steamer. Steam it for 2–2½ hours or until firm to the touch, adding more boiling water to the bottom pan as it evaporates. Turn out the loaf to serve with the tomato sauce. If you like, leave the loaf to cool, garnish it with sliced gherkins and serve it for a picnic or lunch out of doors.

Serves 8

Stuffed Marrow

1 medium-sized marrow	10 ml (2 level teaspoons)
225 g (½ lb) raw minced	thyme, chopped
chicken	5 ml (1 level teaspoon)
1 large onion, finely	marjoram, chopped
chopped	salt and pepper
	tomato sauce (see page 22)

Peel the marrow and cut off a lid at one end. Scoop out the seeds using a long spoon. Steam the marrow and its lid for 10 minutes. Mix the chicken with the onion, thyme, marjoram and plenty of salt and pepper. Moisten it with a few spoons of tomato sauce and pack this stuffing into the marrow, pushing it well down with the handle of a wooden spoon. Put it in a baking dish just long enough to hold the marrow with its lid in place. Pour the remaining tomato sauce over the marrow and bake it at 180°C (350°F)/Gas 4 for about 1 hour. Cut into thick slices and serve each slice with some of the tomato sauce poured over it.

Serves 4–6

Potted Beef

1 kg (2 lb) shin of beef, cubed	salt and pepper
	ground nutmeg
250 ml (½ pint) beef stock	100 g (4 oz) unsalted
2 cloves	butter, melted
1 blade of mace	fresh savory sprigs

Put the meat in a casserole with the stock, cloves, mace and salt and pepper. Cover the casserole and cook the meat at 180°C (350°F)/Gas 4 for about 3–3½ hours or until it is really soft. Remove the cloves and mace and blend the meat and remaining stock until very smooth. Check the seasoning, adding more salt and pepper if necessary and plenty of ground nutmeg. Press this mixture into a large dish and smooth the top. Allow to chill in the fridge. Pour on the melted butter, add a few sprigs of fresh savory and return it to the fridge until it is set. Serve with toast or spread on bread for tea time.

Serves 8

Pork Cheese

2-kg (4-lb) hock of salt
  pork
1 small onion, skinned
2 small carrots, peeled
2 sprigs of thyme
few parsley stalks

1 blade of mace
1 small bay leaf
1 sprig of marjoram or
  oregano
pepper
1 small lettuce, prepared

Put the pork hock in a bowl and cover it with cold water. Leave it to soak for 12 hours. The next day drain it and put it in a pan and cover it with fresh cold water. Bring it to the boil, cover the pan and simmer it for about 3 hours or until the meat is just coming off the bones. Allow it to cool in its liquid until it can be handled. Remove it from the pan and take out the bones and remove the skin. Put the bones and skin in the pan with the onion, carrots, thyme, parsley stalks, mace, bay leaf and marjoram or oregano. Bring to the boil and simmer it, uncovered, until the stock is reduced to about 250 ml (½ pint). Sprinkle pepper over the meat and cut it into fine shreds. Strain the stock over the meat, stir gently, then pour it into a wetted ring mould and leave it to set.

To unmould, dip it up to its rim in hot water for a couple of seconds and turn it out on to a wet plate. Slip it about until it is correctly positioned, then garnish it with the lettuce finely shredded or torn into small pieces.

Serves 8

Glazed Gammon

2·5-kg (5-lb) piece middle
  gammon
2 large onions, quartered
2 large carrots, quartered
1 bay leaf
4 peppercorns

4 sprigs of thyme
60 ml (4 level tablespoons)
  jelly marmalade
60 ml (4 tablespoons) honey
few drops tabasco sauce
whole cloves

Wipe the gammon and put it in a large pan. Just cover it with cold water, bring it to the boil and pour off the liquid. Cover with fresh cold water, add the onions, carrots, bay leaf, peppercorns and thyme and bring slowly to the boil. Cover the pan and simmer it for 1 hour, then drain off the water. As soon as the joint is cool enough to handle, strip off the skin and wrap the joint in foil. Put the gammon in a baking tin and cook it at 180°C (350°F)/Gas 4 for 30 minutes.

Meanwhile, blend the marmalade with the honey and a few drops of tabasco, just enough to spice the mixture pleasantly. Remove the gammon from the oven, take off the foil and score the fat into small diamonds. Brush with some of the marmalade mixture and return it to the oven at 220°C (425°F)/Gas 7 for 10 minutes, then brush again with marmalade and return to the oven for another 10 minutes. Brush once more with marmalade, stud the centres of the diamonds with the cloves and return the gammon to the oven for the last 10 minutes' cooking time, when it should be crisp and golden on top. Remove and allow to cool completely.

Serves 16

Poultry Vol-au-Vents

369-g (13-oz) packet frozen puff pastry	béchamel sauce (see page 30)
225 g (8 oz) cooked turkey, chopped	100 g (4 oz) button mushroom caps
100 g (4 oz) cooked ham, chopped	50 g (2 oz) butter
salt and pepper	15 ml (1 level tablespoon) tarragon, finely chopped

Allow the pastry to thaw at room temperature for 1 hour or more, then roll it on a lightly-floured board to just less than a 1·25-cm (½-in) thickness. Use a 5-cm (2-in) cutter to cut out 16 vol-au-vents. Using a 2·5-cm (1-in) cutter, cut out lids from the vol-au-vents, pressing no more than half-way through the pastry. Transfer the vol-au-vents to wet baking trays and bake them at 230°C (450°F)/Gas 8 for about 20 minutes until golden brown and well risen. Remove from the oven and, with the tip of a knife, remove the lids. If any of the cases have risen unevenly, press them down gently while still hot to make them more even. Allow to cool and then, with the tip of the knife, remove any soft uncooked mixture from the centres of the cases.

Mix the turkey and ham with salt and pepper and stir them into the béchamel sauce. Fry the mushroom caps lightly in the butter for about 5 minutes, turning them all the time. Remove and drain on kitchen paper. Stir the tarragon into the sauce, check the seasoning and add more salt and pepper if necessary. Spoon this mixture into the cases, top with the mushroom caps, and finish with the pastry lids. Serve hot.

Serves 8

Galantine of Chicken

1·5-kg (3-lb) chicken	lemon rind, finely grated
salt and pepper	1 litre (2 pints) good
1 kg (2 lb) sausagemeat	chicken stock
2 hard-boiled eggs,	250 ml ($\frac{1}{2}$ pint) mayonnaise
chopped	(see page 40)
25 g (1 oz) pistachio nuts,	250 ml ($\frac{1}{2}$ pint) packet aspic
blanched	mustard and cress, prepared
100 g (4 oz) tongue	2·5-cm (1-in) piece cucumber
5 ml (1 level teaspoon)	

Rinse the chicken inside and out and place it on a board with its back upwards. Cut through the skin and flesh from the neck to the tail. It's important to use a small sharp knife to remove the carcass; a blunt knife will make it difficult to keep the meat all in one piece. Holding the blade of the knife close to the bones, cut away the flesh and skin on both sides until you come to the wings and legs. Don't worry if you miss some of the flesh; you can always go back later, trim it off and add it to the galantine. When you come to the leg and wing on one side, work all round one at a time, keeping the knife close to the bone and peeling off the flesh like a coat sleeve, inside out. Once this is done, work round the breast until you reach the other leg and wing. Treat them as before. Then continue until the carcass is free. Trim good pieces of flesh off the carcass and use the bones to make a good rich stock in which to cook the finished galantine.

Lay the complete piece of chicken flat on a board, skin side down, and distribute the pieces of flesh evenly, then flatten the whole thing with a rolling pin. Sprinkle well with salt and pepper. Mash the sausagemeat to make it smooth and spread it over the chicken almost to the edges. Sprinkle the chopped eggs in two lines either side of the centre. Chop the nuts and tongue and arrange the nuts in two lines either side of the eggs with the tongue pieces in the centre. Sprinkle with the lemon rind and some salt and pepper. Season well again. Fold in the sides to meet in the middle, then fold the galantine in half, making a 'seam' on one side. Wrap the galantine in a large piece of muslin, securing the ends well with pieces of string, rather like a large boiled sweet.

Bring the stock to the boil in a pan large enough to hold the galantine and lower it in. Lower the heat, cover the pan and simmer it for 2–2½ hours. Lift it out carefully when cooked and remove the muslin. Wrap it in a clean piece of muslin and secure it tightly in a good shape. Place it between 2 oval dishes, weight the top one and leave it until it is quite cold.

When you unwrap the galantine the second time, put it, best side up, on a wire rack with a large plate underneath. Make the mayonnaise and the packet aspic and when the aspic is almost on the point of setting, stir half of it into the mayonnaise. Allow to thicken but not set, then pour it all over the galantine in one smooth flowing coat. Gather up the drips and repeat the coat if necessary after the first one has set. Dip a few sprigs of mustard and cress in the liquid aspic (kept liquid by standing the bowl over a pan of hot water) and arrange them on the galantine. Run the tines of a fork down the skin of the cucumber to crimp it and cut it into see-through slices. Arrange these, after dipping them in the liquid aspic, down the centre of the galantine. Allow to set, then coat with a layer of liquid aspic and leave to set. Serve cut into slices.

Serves 8

Fricassée of Veal

0·5 kg (1 lb) veal fillet
1 medium-sized onion,
  skinned
6 button mushrooms
2 sprigs of thyme
few parsley stalks
1 blade of mace
6 peppercorns
salt

velouté sauce (see page 68)
5 ml (1 teaspoon) lemon
  juice, strained
pepper
croûtons (see page 34)
30 ml (2 tablespoons)
  double cream
parsley sprigs

Wipe the meat and cut it into 2·5-cm (1-in) squares. Put them into a saucepan and pour in water almost to cover. Bring to the boil and skim. Now add the onion, mushrooms, thyme, parsley stalks, mace, peppercorns and a good pinch of salt. Simmer for 1 hour or until tender, then strain off and keep the stock. Discard the peppercorns, mace, herbs, mushrooms and onion.

Make the velouté sauce, but use 250 ml ($\frac{1}{2}$ pint) reserved veal stock. Bring to the boil and simmer for 2 minutes, then stir in the lemon juice, salt and pepper. Add the meat to the sauce and reheat it gently, checking the seasoning.

Make the croûtons from thin slices of white bread but cut them into crescents rather than cubes. Stir the cream into the fricassée and garnish it with the croûtons and parsley sprigs.

Serves 4

Chicken in a Basket

6 chicken drumsticks
30 ml (2 tablespoons)
  cooking oil
15 ml (1 tablespoon) soy
  sauce
1 small onion, finely
  chopped

salt and pepper
plain flour
1 large egg, beaten
150 g (6 oz) fresh white
  breadcrumbs
1 clove garlic, crushed
oil for deep frying

Wipe the chicken drumsticks and arrange them in one layer in a baking dish. Whisk the oil with the soy sauce, onion and plenty of salt and pepper and pour this mixture over the chicken. Allow to marinate for 1 hour, turning them frequently. Remove them from the marinade and drain them on kitchen paper. Season the flour with salt and pepper and use to dust the chicken. Coat with beaten egg. Stir the breadcrumbs and garlic together until well mixed, then use this to coat the chicken, pressing the crumbs on well and shaking off the excess.

Heat the oil to 182°C (360°F) or until a 2·5-cm (1-in) cube of bread rises to the surface and browns in 1 minute. Cook 3 drumsticks at a time, lowering them in gently and frying them for 15 minutes. Don't use a wire basket because it makes square marks on the finished dish. Drain on kitchen paper, and serve in a wicker basket.

Serves 6

Chicken Chaudfroid

1·5-kg (3-lb) chicken
few parsley stalks
3 sprigs of thyme
1 blade of mace
12 peppercorns
1 small bay leaf
1 small piece lemon rind

250 ml (½ pint) packet
　aspic
béchamel sauce (see page
　30)
radishes, lemon rind,
　cucumber skin and dill
　or fennel for garnish
1 small lettuce, prepared

Rinse the chicken inside and out and put it in a large sauce-pan with the parsley stalks, thyme, mace, peppercorns, bay leaf and lemon rind. Add enough cold water to cover the chicken and bring it slowly to the boil. Lower the heat, cover the pan and simmer for 1 hour or until the bird is tender. Check it by pushing a knife blade into the thickest part of one of the legs. Remove it from the cooking liquid and allow to cool. As soon as it is cool enough to handle, remove the skin and transfer the chicken to a cake rack with a plate underneath to finish cooling completely. Just before decorating the chicken, pour off any liquid that has collected underneath it. Put a clean plate under the chicken.

Make up the packet aspic as directed and make the béch-amel sauce. Allow the aspic to cool almost to its setting point, then stir half of it into the béchamel sauce and allow it to thicken slightly but not set. Check the consistency by pouring some over the back of a wooden spoon. When it coats the spoon well but still smoothly, pour it all over the chicken in one smooth flowing coat. The plate underneath will catch all the drips. Allow to set and if you're not com-pletely happy with this coat, gather up all the drips and put them back into the bowl. Stir the béchamel and aspic sauce very gently over a pan of hot water until the consistency is again right but don't let the sauce become too hot. Repeat the flowing coat and allow to set.

When set, stir the remaining plain aspic over a pan of hot water until it is liquid. Cut thin slices from the radishes, tiny circles from the lemon rind and stalks and leaves from the cucumber skin. Using a hat pin, dip each piece of decoration in the liquid aspic and place it on the chicken to form a spray of flowers. Use sprigs of dill or fennel for more decoration. When the decorations have set in place, pour the remaining aspic all over the chicken and allow it to set.

Serves 6–8

Stuffed Tomatoes Turkish Style

25 g (1 oz) butter
75 g (3 oz) long-grain rice
125 ml (¼ pint) hot water
225 g (½ lb) raw mince
1 large onion, skinned
salt and pepper
ground cumin

15 ml (1 level tablespoon)
  parsley, chopped
8 large tomatoes
250 ml (½ pint) good
  chicken stock
5 ml (1 level teaspoon)
  dill, roughly chopped

Melt the butter in a frying pan and fry the rice for 2 minutes, then pour on the hot water and cook the rice fast, stirring, until it is dry and all the water has been absorbed. Put the mince in a bowl, grate in the onion and season the meat well with salt and pepper. Add the rice, ground cumin to taste and the chopped parsley and mix well together. Cut a third off each tomato to use as a lid. Using a teaspoon, scoop out the centres and mix them into the mince filling. Use this mixture to stuff the tomatoes and arrange them in a baking dish in one layer. Pour in enough stock to come half-way up the tomatoes. Top each one with its lid and bake them at 180°C (350°F)/Gas 4 for about 30 minutes or until cooked but still keeping their shape. Serve sprinkled with the dill and spoon a little of the stock on to each tomato as it is served.

Serves 4

Chinese Spare Ribs

1 kg (2 lb) pork spare ribs	*Red sauce:*
1 large onion, chopped	45 ml (3 tablespoons) soy
pepper	sauce
30 ml (2 tablespoons)	15 ml (1 tablespoon) sherry
sherry	15 ml (1 tablespoon)
45 ml (3 tablespoons) soy	chicken stock (reserved)
sauce	pinch of caster sugar
½ chicken stock cube	5 ml (1 level teaspoon)
250 ml (½ pint) boiling	lemon rind, finely grated
water	5 ml (1 level teaspoon)
	onion, finely chopped

Rinse the spare ribs and put them in a large pan. Just cover them with cold water, bring them to the boil and cook them for 10 minutes. Drain and cut them into individual ribs. Return the ribs to a saucepan, add the onion and sprinkle with plenty of freshly ground black pepper. Add the sherry, soy sauce and all but 15 ml (1 tablespoon) of the chicken stock cube dissolved in the boiling water. Cover the pan and simmer the ribs for 45 minutes to 1 hour, turning them several times, and keeping an eye on them towards the end of the cooking time because they should be almost dry. Meanwhile, make the red sauce by putting all the ingredients in a small pan, bringing them slowly to the boil, then simmering them for about 15 minutes, stirring frequently.

Transfer the spare ribs to a meat tin, arranging them in one layer. Brush them liberally with the red sauce and cook them at 200°C (400°F)/Gas 6 for about 15 minutes. Serve hot.

Serves 4–8

Cutlets in Pastry Jackets

6 lean lamb cutlets
salt and pepper
30 ml (2 level tablespoons)
  chutney

shortcrust pastry (see page
  67)
1 standard egg, beaten

Wipe the cutlets and trim off the excess fat. Scrape the bones to remove any small pieces of meat. Season the cutlets with salt and pepper and spread each one with a little of the chutney.

Roll the pastry thinly, then cut out six 13-cm (5-in) rounds. Put one cutlet on each pastry round with the curved side near one edge. Moisten the edge and fold the pastry over to enclose the cutlet but leave the bone sticking out, then seal the edges at the side. Trim them and decorate the edge by crimping. Left-over pieces of pastry can be used to decorate the cutlets, sticking them in place with a little of the beaten egg. Wrap pieces of foil around the exposed bones to keep them white during cooking. Arrange all the cutlets on a greased baking tray, brush them with egg and bake them at 200°C (400°F)/Gas 6 for about 40 minutes until they are golden brown. Add a cutlet frill to each bone to help when eating them by hand and serve with salads. The cutlets can be eaten hot or cold.

Serves 6

Moussaka

2 large aubergines, sliced
salt
olive oil
2 large onions, finely
  chopped
1 kg (2 lb) raw mince
10 ml (2 level teaspoons)
  oregano, chopped

5 ml (1 level teaspoon)
  ground nutmeg
30 ml (2 tablespoons)
  tomato paste
pepper
plain flour
500 ml (1 pint) béchamel
  sauce (see page 30)
50 g (2 oz) Cheddar cheese,
  grated

Layer the aubergine slices in a colander with a good sprinkling of salt to each layer. Put a small plate on top and weight the plate, then leave the aubergines to drain for about 1 hour. Heat 30 ml (2 tablespoons) oil in a frying pan and add the onions. Fry them for 5 minutes, then stir in the mince and continue to cook, stirring, until the mince is brown all over. Stir in the oregano, nutmeg, tomato paste, salt and pepper and 250 ml ($\frac{1}{2}$ pint) cold water and continue to simmer the mince for another 30 minutes.

Meanwhile, rinse the aubergines to remove the salt, drain them and dry them on kitchen paper. Dust each slice with flour and fry them, a few at a time, in hot oil until golden on both sides. Drain on kitchen paper. Now make the béchamel sauce. Stir 60 ml (4 tablespoons) of the sauce into the mince and check the seasoning of both, adding more salt, pepper and nutmeg if necessary.

Layer the aubergine slices, mince and sauce in this order in a deep baking dish, finishing with a good layer of sauce. Sprinkle with the cheese and bake the moussaka at 190°C (375°F)/Gas 5 for about 40 minutes until the top is golden brown.

Serves 4

Fruits

The short season of the summer fruits makes it all the more sweet. After enjoying the first few bowls of strawberries and the superior raspberries, when it seems wrong to do more than sprinkle them with sugar and cover them with thick cream, you can use them as a flavouring rather than as a whole berry. Whisked with cream into a purée for fools, mousses and cold soufflés, crushed lightly for fruity sauces, or blended with a rich custard for ice creams, all the soft fruits are a treat. The other summer fruits – the apricot, the peach and the cherry – will, unless very ripe, need a little stewing to turn them into a smooth consistency.

Some avocado recipes have crept in here. Technically it is a fruit and although we tend to serve the avocado only as a starter, its rich and creamy flavour blends perfectly with creams and jellies to make puddings of an unusual taste and texture. An avocado mousse is a good addition to a summer buffet table, adding its delicate green colour to the pinks of most summer puddings. Cream cheese sweets go well with the soft fruits and I've included a recipe for coeur à la crème – cream cheese hearts from France with a raspberry sauce – and a magnificent cheesecake, sandwiched together with a luscious strawberry filling.

Raspberry Water Ice

225 g (8 oz) granulated
  sugar
0·5 kg (1 lb) raspberries,
  prepared

2 large egg whites, whisked
15 g ($\frac{1}{2}$ oz) caster sugar

Put the granulated sugar and 250 ml ($\frac{1}{2}$ pint) cold water in a pan and heat gently until the sugar has dissolved. Bring to the boil and boil the mixture for about 5 minutes until it is syrupy. Meanwhile, rinse the raspberries and reserve some of the best berries for decoration. Put the rest in a pan with 45 ml (3 tablespoons) cold water and heat gently until the raspberries start to soften and the juice runs. Push them through a nylon sieve to remove the seeds. Whisk the sugar syrup and raspberry purée together, pour the mixture into a plastic box and put it in the freezer or in the ice-making compartment of the fridge for about 2 hours until it is half-frozen.

Remove from the freezer and turn the ice into a bowl. Whisk it well and fold in all but a little of the egg whites. Return it to the plastic box and return to the freezer for 3–4 hours or until it is solid. Meanwhile, dip the reserved raspberries in the reserved egg white to coat them well, then scatter the caster sugar over them to coat. Allow to dry. Serve the raspberry water ice in pretty glasses decorated with the frosted fruits.

Serves 4

Strawberry Ice Cream

225 g (8 oz) strawberries, prepared
90 ml (6 tablespoons) vodka

142-g (5-oz) carton double cream, whipped
50 g (2 oz) caster sugar

Rinse the berries, put them in a bowl and pour on the vodka. Leave them for 1 hour, then mash them to a purée. Put it into a plastic box and then into the freezer or ice-making compartment of your fridge and freeze until half-frozen, which will take about 1½ hours. Turn the fruit into a bowl and whisk it well until it is smooth. Fold in the cream and sugar and return it to the box and the freezer until it is solid. If you want to make a very smooth ice cream, take it out again before it is completely frozen and whisk it well for a couple of minutes, then freeze until solid. Spoon into glasses and serve.

Serves 4

Rich Vanilla Ice Cream

250 ml (½ pint) milk
75 g (3 oz) caster sugar
2 large eggs, beaten

vanilla essence
250 ml (½ pint) double cream, half-whipped

Heat the milk with the caster sugar until it has dissolved, but don't let it boil. Pour it on to the beaten eggs, stirring all the time, then stand the bowl over a saucepan of gently simmering water and stir it over a gentle heat until the custard thickens. Strain it into a plastic box to be used for freezing and stir in 10 ml (2 teaspoons) vanilla essence. Allow to cool completely in the fridge with a piece of wet greaseproof paper pressed close to the surface of the custard to prevent a skin forming.

Fold in the half-whipped cream and put the ice cream in

the freezer or the ice-making compartment of your fridge for 3–4 hours until it is frozen.

Serves 8

Chocolate Ice Cream

125 ml (¼ pint) milk
40 g (1½ oz) caster sugar
1 large egg, beaten

100 g (4 oz) plain
   chocolate, grated
142-g (5-oz) carton double
   cream, half-whipped

Heat the milk with the caster sugar, but don't let it boil. When the sugar has dissolved, pour it on to the egg, stirring all the time. Cook over a very gentle heat until the custard thickens, then strain it into a plastic box for freezing. Press a piece of wet greaseproof paper close to the surface of the custard and allow to cool in the fridge. When cold, melt the chocolate and stir it into the custard with the half-whipped cream. Freeze for 3–4 hours and scoop into glasses to serve.

Serves 4

Apricot Fruit Cream

0·5 kg (1 lb) apricots,
   stoned
75 g (3 oz) caster sugar

250 ml (½ pint) double
   cream, half-whipped
30 ml (2 tablespoons) rum

Reserve 6 apricots and put the rest into a saucepan with 250 ml (½ pint) cold water and the caster sugar. Bring slowly to the boil, then simmer for 30 minutes or until the apricots are soft enough to purée. Push them through a sieve and allow to cool. Fold in the half-whipped cream and pour this mixture into a plastic box for freezing. Freeze for 2 hours until half-frozen.

Meanwhile, finely chop the reserved apricot halves. Use the ripest ones for this because they won't be cooked. Put them in a bowl, pour on the rum and leave them to soak for 2 hours. Remove the ice cream, turn it into a bowl and whisk it for 1 minute. Fold in the apricot pieces and the rum and return the ice cream to the freezer until solid.

Serves 6

Currant Sorbet

0·5 kg (1 lb) black, red or mixed currants, prepared

225 g (8 oz) granulated sugar

Mash the currants to a purée, then push it through a sieve to remove the skins and seeds. Put the sugar in a pan with 250 ml (½ pint) cold water and heat gently until the sugar has dissolved. Bring to the boil and boil hard for 5 minutes. Leave until it is quite cold, then whisk it with the currant purée, pour the mixture into a plastic box and put it in the freezer or ice-making compartment of the fridge for about 1 hour or until it is half-frozen. Remove and whisk well, then return to the box and freeze until solid.

Serves 6

Mint Cream

100 g (4 oz) granulated sugar
36 mint leaves, washed

juice of 1 lemon, strained
125 ml (¼ pint) double cream, half-whipped

Put the sugar with 125 ml (¼ pint) cold water in a small pan and heat it gently until the sugar has dissolved, then boil hard for 5 minutes until it is syrupy. In an electric blender, blend the mint leaves with this sugar syrup, blend in the lemon juice and pour the mixture into a plastic box. Put it in the freezer or in the ice-making compartment of your fridge and leave to freeze for about 1 hour or until it is half-frozen. Return it to the blender and blend well, then blend in the half-whipped cream. Pour the mixture back into the plastic box and return it to the freezer to freeze until solid.

Other herb ice creams may be made in the same way; lemon thyme and lemon balm are particularly successful.

Serves 6

Peaches in White Wine

8 large peaches
250 ml (½ pint) dry white
　wine
75 g (3 oz) caster sugar
50 g (2 oz) sugar lumps
1 large lemon
10 ml (2 level teaspoons)
　arrowroot

It's best to use slightly under-ripe peaches for this dish. Skin the peaches by pouring boiling water over them; when the skins split, gently peel them off. Put the peaches into an ovenproof dish, pour on the wine, 250 ml (½ pint) cold water and stir in the sugar. Cover the dish with a piece of foil and bake at 180°C (350°F)/Gas 4 for about 30 minutes.

Meanwhile, rub the sugar lumps over the lemon until the sugar has absorbed the oil and is yellow on all sides. Squeeze out and strain the lemon juice. Remove the peaches from the wine and put them in a serving dish. Blend the arrowroot with a little cold water. Pour on the hot syrup, stirring all the time, and heat it gently in a small pan until it has thickened and cleared. Stir in the lemon juice and pour it over the peaches. Crush the sugar lumps with a rolling pin, sprinkle them over the peaches and serve at once.

Serves 8

Cherry Clafouti

0·75 kg (1½ lb) cherries,
  stoned
3 large eggs, beaten
45 ml (3 level tablespoons)
  plain flour
pinch of salt

75 ml (5 level tablespoons)
  caster sugar
375 ml (¾ pint) milk,
  lukewarm
25 g (1 oz) butter

Wash the cherries, drain them well and dry them on a tea towel. Whisk the eggs and flour together with a pinch of salt, then stir in 45 ml (3 level tablespoons) sugar. Pour on the lukewarm milk, whisking all the time. Butter a large shallow ovenproof dish and put in the cherries. Pour on the batter and bake at 220°C (425°F)/Gas 7 for about 25 minutes or until the cherries have risen to the top and the batter is set and golden. Sprinkle with the remaining sugar and serve warm.

Serves 6

Raspberry Pavlova

3 large egg whites, whisked
pinch of salt
175 g (6 oz) caster sugar
5 ml (1 teaspoon) vinegar
5 ml (1 teaspoon) vanilla
  essence

225 g (8 oz) raspberries,
  prepared
142-g (5-oz) carton double
  cream, whipped

Whisk the egg whites with the pinch of salt until they are very stiff. Fold in the sugar with the vinegar and vanilla essence and spoon the mixture quickly into a piping bag fitted with a large star nozzle. Pipe the mixture into a large circle on non-stick paper on a baking tray, then build up the sides with another 2 circles and top with a row of stars. Using the last of the mixture, fill in the base and smooth gently with a palette knife if there are any spaces left. Bake at 150°C (300°F)/Gas 2 for 1–1½ hours until firm. Leave to cool on the tray, then carefully remove the paper and put the Pavlova on a serving plate. Fill with half the raspberries, reserving the best for the top. Spread with the cream and top with the reserved raspberries. Serve at once.

Serves 8

Apricot Marshmallow

10 ml (2 level teaspoons) powdered gelatine
125 ml (¼ pint) warm water
2 large egg whites, whisked

45 ml (3 level tablespoons) caster sugar
225 g (8 oz) apricots, stoned

Put the gelatine in a bowl, pour on the warm water and let it dissolve standing in a pan of gently simmering water. When it is clear and while it is hot, pour it on to the stiffly beaten egg whites and whisk until the mixture looks like whipped cream. Stir in the sugar. Mash the apricots to a purée and stir them into the mixture. Whisk for 2–3 minutes and serve piled into glasses.

Serves 4

Peach and Redcurrant Dreams

4 large ripe peaches
100 g (4 oz) redcurrants, prepared

50 g (2 oz) caster sugar
250 ml (½ pint) double cream, whipped

Put the peaches in a bowl, pour on boiling water and when the skins split, peel them off gently. Cut the peaches into slices, removing the stones, and then into small chunks.

Put the redcurrants in a small pan with 60 ml (4 table-spoons) cold water and bring slowly to the boil. When the redcurrants first start to split, remove them from the heat, gently stir in the sugar so that you don't break them and allow them to cool in the fridge. Mix them with the peaches and stir the fruit and juice into the whipped cream. Serve with boudoir biscuits in tiny glasses.

Serves 8

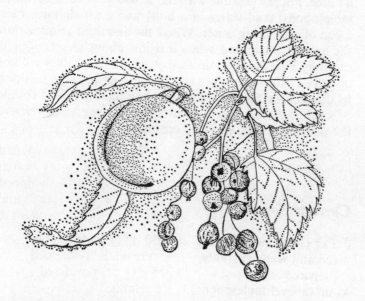

Apricot Suédoise

175 g (6 oz) caster sugar
strip of lemon rind
1 kg (2 lb) apricots, stoned
12 whole blanched almonds

25 g (1 oz) powdered gelatine
juice of 1 lemon, strained

Put the sugar in a small pan with the lemon rind and 375 ml (¾ pint) cold water. Heat gently until the sugar has dissolved, then boil it hard for 15 minutes until it is syrupy. Rinse the apricots and put them in the sugar syrup. Bring the syrup and apricots to the boil, then lower the heat, cover the pan and poach the fruit gently until it is tender. Remove 12 of the best apricot halves and allow them to drain on kitchen paper. Place an almond in the hollow of each half and arrange them cut sides down in a 15-cm (6-in) cake tin with a fixed base. Discard the lemon rind and push the remaining apricots and the syrup through a sieve to make a purée. Put the gelatine with the lemon juice and 30 ml (2 tablespoons) cold water in a bowl and let it dissolve over a pan of simmering water. Whisk the dissolved gelatine into the apricot purée and when it is just about to set, pour it carefully into the cake tin so that the apricot halves are not disturbed. Allow to set in a cool place. Unmould the suédoise by dipping the tin up to its rim in boiling water for a couple of seconds, then put a plate over the tin, invert and remove the tin. Serve with whipped cream.

Serves 8

Currant Soufflé

0·5 kg (1 lb) mixed black, red and white currants, prepared
45 ml (3 level tablespoons) granulated sugar
4 large eggs
175 g (6 oz) caster sugar

250 ml (½ pint) double cream, half-whipped
15 g (½ oz) powdered gelatine
45 ml (3 tablespoons) warm water

Rinse the currants and put them in a pan with the granulated sugar and 125 ml (¼ pint) cold water. Heat slowly until the sugar has dissolved, then simmer until the berries break and soften. Push them through a sieve to make a purée and to remove the pips. Put the eggs with the caster sugar in a large bowl. Whisk until the mixture is light and fluffy. If you have an electric whisk there is no need to put the bowl over a pan of simmering water, but if whisking by hand it speeds up the process. Make sure the bowl does not touch the water. Remove from the heat and whisk until the bowl and mixture are quite cold. Fold in the currant purée. Half-whip the cream and fold it into the currant mixture. Dissolve the gelatine in the warm water in a bowl standing in a pan of gently simmering water. When it is clear, whisk it into the mixture.

Wrap a collar of greaseproof paper round a 15-cm (6-in) soufflé dish to stand 5 cm (2 in) higher than the dish and secure it with transparent adhesive tape. When the mixture is on the point of setting, pour it into the soufflé dish and leave it to set in a cool place. When set, carefully peel off the paper collar and decorate if liked with sprigs of red-currants, rinsed and dried but still on their stalks.

Serves 8

Strawberry Cheesecake

40 g (1½ oz) semi-sweet
  biscuits, crushed
pinch of ground mace
15 g (½ oz) butter, melted
4 large eggs, separated
175 g (7 oz) caster sugar
0·5 kg (1 lb) soft cream
  cheese
40 g (1½ oz) plain flour

30 ml (2 tablespoons)
  lemon juice, strained
250 ml (½ pint) double
  cream, whipped
0·5 kg (1 lb) strawberries,
  prepared
90 ml (6 level tablespoons)
  redcurrant jelly
15 ml (1 level tablespoon)
  arrowroot

Mix the biscuits with the ground mace. Brush the butter liberally over the base and sides of a 20-cm (8-in) cake tin with a loose base. Dust all over with the biscuit crumbs and shake out excess. Whisk the egg yolks in a large bowl, then add the sugar and continue beating until the mixture is thick and fluffy. Break down the cream cheese with a fork until it is really soft and beat it into the egg yolks with the flour, lemon juice and cream. Whisk the egg whites until stiff but not dry and fold them into the cream cheese mixture. Pour this mixture into the prepared tin and bake at 120°C (250°F)/Gas ½ for about 1½ hours. Turn off the oven and leave the cheesecake for 2 hours without opening the door. Then remove it and let it cool in the tin.

Push up the loose base and cut the cheesecake into 3 layers, then slide the bottom layer on to a serving plate. Halve the strawberries and arrange a third of them over each of the three layers. Heat the redcurrant jelly in a small pan. Blend the arrowroot with a little cold water, pour in some of the hot jelly, stir it and return it to the pan. Bring to the boil and cook until the jelly is thick and clear. Spoon a little over the bottom layer, add the middle layer, spoon on some more redcurrant glaze and top with the remaining layer. Spoon the rest of the glaze over the top layer, letting it trickle down the sides. Leave to set for 30 minutes before serving.

Serves 8–10

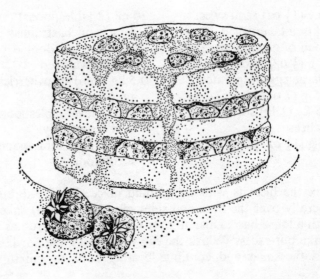

Cherry Fool

0·5 kg (1 lb) Morello
  cherries, stoned
175 g (6 oz) caster sugar
2·5-cm (1-in) cinnamon
  stick

30 ml (2 tablespoons)
  cherry brandy
250 ml ($\frac{1}{2}$ pint) double
  cream, whipped

Put the cherries with the sugar and cinnamon in a pan. Add 125 ml ($\frac{1}{4}$ pint) cold water and bring slowly to the boil. Make sure the sugar has dissolved, then simmer the cherries until they are really soft. Push them through a sieve to make a purée. Taste for sweetness, adding more sugar if necessary. Add the cherry brandy, then stir in the whipped cream to give a marbled effect. Spoon into glasses and serve.

Serves 6–8

June Fool

0·5 kg (1 lb) gooseberries
50 g (2 oz) caster sugar
1 large soft avocado

green vegetable colouring
  (optional)

Top and tail the gooseberries and simmer them in very little water until almost cooked. Remove a few of the best berries for decoration, then continue cooking the remainder until they are soft enough to mash to a purée. Stir in the sugar. Peel the avocado using a stainless steel knife, cut it in half and remove the stone. Mash the flesh to a purée and combine with the gooseberry mixture. (If you prefer, you can put the gooseberries in a blender, and purée them together). Add a few drops of green colouring if liked and divide between individual dishes. Decorate with the reserved gooseberries and chill before serving.

Serves 4

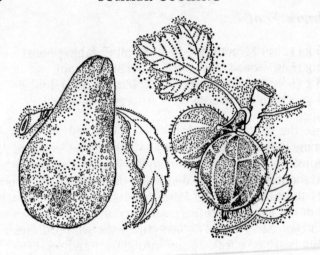

Avocado Pudding

1 568-ml (1-pint) packet   125 ml (¼ pint) double
    lemon jelly   cream
1 large soft avocado   strawberries for decoration

Dissolve the lemon jelly in 375 ml (¾ pint) hot water. Using
a stainless steel knife, peel the avocado, cut it in half, remove
the stone and mash the flesh to a fine purée. Whisk the
purée into the jelly with the double cream and continue
whisking for 1 minute. Allow the mixture almost to set (in
the kitchen, not the fridge), then whisk again for a couple of
minutes until it is light and fluffy. Transfer it to a mould or
4 or 6 individual dishes and leave to set. Turn out and
decorate with strawberries.

Serves 4–6

Summer Pudding

225 g (½ lb) raspberries	100 g (4 oz) granulated
225 g (½ lb) redcurrants	sugar
225 g (½ lb) blackcurrants	juice of 1 lemon, strained
225 g (½ lb) strawberries	12 slices white bread

Rinse the fruit and remove hulls, stalks and any damaged berries. Put them into a large saucepan with 60 ml (4 tablespoons) cold water and simmer them gently until they are soft and cooked. Stir in the sugar, but stir gently because the fruit is best if it's not too broken up. Allow to cool, then stir in the lemon juice.

Cut the crusts off the bread and cut one slice into a round to fit the bottom of a basin. Cut some of the other slices into wedge-shaped pieces and fit them together to line the sides of the basin. Fill with the fruit and juice, packing the pudding. Top with the remaining pieces of bread, covering the fruit completely. Put a small plate on the pudding, small enough to go inside the basin, and top it with all the weights from your scales or with two or three large tins of fruit. Leave it in the fridge overnight. Next day, turn it on to a serving plate. Decorate it with fresh fruit and sprigs of mint and serve cut into wedges with lots of double cream.

Serves 6–8

Coeur à la Crème

0·5 kg (1 lb) good cream	225 g (½ lb) raspberries,
cheese	hulled
2 large egg whites	25 g (1 oz) caster sugar
60 ml (4 tablespoons)	
double cream	

Break down the cream cheese with a fork. Whisk the egg whites until stiff and fold them into the cream cheese with the double cream to make a soft but not too runny cream. Wet pieces of kitchen paper and use them to line 6 heart-shaped coeur à la crème moulds, or 2 large sieves. Spoon the cream mixture into the moulds or the sieves and put them in the fridge to set. It's wise to put a plate underneath in case they drip a little. Once set, put them in the freezer or the freezing compartment of the fridge for 30 minutes to make them easier to turn out and position on the plate. Turn them out and remove the paper. If they've got marks on them you can remove these by dipping one finger in a little water and smoothing it over them.

Crush the raspberries with the sugar and leave them for 30 minutes for the juice to run. Tip this sauce over the moulds and serve when they have softened to room temperature.

Serves 6

Bazaars

Excellent work is done all over the country by people organising bazaars, fêtes, summer fairs and carnivals to provide money for charity. The most popular stall with the adults is always the one piled high with home-made produce. I've done my share of making pounds and pounds of preserves to be sold for a good cause and if you've been earmarked for this particular job, you'll find lots of recipes in the preserves chapter. But if you can choose, home-made biscuits and sweets provide the biggest return of cash on the time taken to produce them and with the modest outlay of a few shillings on some cellophane bags and narrow, pretty ribbon you can, with justification, charge a pence or two more for your packets. However, if you're going to set to and do a day's baking, you'll have to choose a quiet time or, I suspect, the family will discover needier charities right at home. Some recipes provide a lot of scope for variation and you can set up an assembly line of mixing, working,

113

baking and bagging without getting bored. If, for instance, you want to make up a multi-coloured batch of sweets from the recipe for peppermint creams, you can add oil of lemon and yellow colouring to one batch, almond essence and pink colouring to another and violet essence and colouring to a third. Fudge can also be varied. Besides the vanilla, chocolate and fruit and nut, you can add snipped marsh-mallows, chopped glacé cherries, dates, orange and lemon rinds, and walnuts to a coffee-flavoured fudge. Biscuits, too, lend themselves to a variety of additions – try different spices, orange or lemon rinds, coffee, almonds, caraway seeds, nuts and essences.

Gingerbread Men

325 g (12 oz) golden syrup
275 g (10 oz) caster sugar
25 ml (5 level teaspoons)
  ground ginger
5 ml (1 level teaspoon)
  ground cinnamon
275 g (10 oz) margarine

45 ml (3 level tablespoons)
  bicarbonate of soda
1·13 kg (2½ lb) plain flour
good pinch of salt
2 large eggs, beaten
225 g (8 oz) icing sugar,
  sifted
1 large egg white, whisked

Put the golden syrup, caster sugar, ginger and cinnamon in a large pan and heat them gently until the sugar has melted. Add the margarine and stir until melted. Stir in the bicarbonate of soda and leave to cool for 5 minutes. Sift the flour and salt together and mix them into the syrup mixture with the beaten whole eggs. Mix to a smooth dough. Knead it until it is smooth and pliable and divide it in half to roll it out. Roll to a 0·5-cm (¼-in) thickness and, using a gingerbread man cutter, cut out shapes. Arrange them on greased baking trays, and bake them at 180°C (350°F)/Gas 4 for 15–20 minutes or until golden. Cool on the trays for 5 minutes, then remove with a palette knife and cool on wire racks.

Gradually beat the icing sugar into the whisked egg white and continue beating until the icing is thick and glossy. Put it into a piping bag with a fine writing pipe and pipe eyes, nose, mouth, buttons and any other features on the ginger-bread men. Allow to set.

Makes 16–18

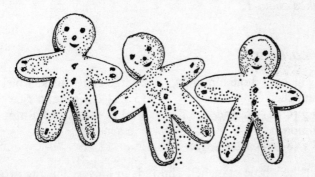

Viennese Cookies

275 g (10 oz) butter
175 g (6 oz) icing sugar
175 g (6 oz) plain flour
50 g (2 oz) cornflour
pinch of salt
angelica
glacé cherries, halved

100 g (4 oz) plain chocolate, melted
25 g (1 oz) chopped almonds, toasted
25 g (1 oz) chocolate vermicelli

Cream 225 g (8 oz) butter with 50 g (2 oz) icing sugar until light and fluffy. Sift the flour, cornflour and salt and fold these dry ingredients into the creamed butter, using a large metal spoon. Spoon the mixture into a large piping bag fitted with a large star pipe, and pipe circles, stars, fingers and shells on greased baking trays. Decorate the circles with diamond shapes cut from the angelica and the stars with halves of glacé cherry. Bake them at 190°C (375°F)/Gas 5 for 12–15 minutes or until pale golden brown. Remove and cool on wire racks.

Cream the remaining butter and icing sugar and spoon it into a small piping bag fitted with a small star pipe. Pipe butter cream on half the fingers and shells and sandwich with the other half. Dip the ends of the fingers in the melted chocolate, then in toasted almonds, and leave to set. Dip the ends of the shells first in chocolate and then in chocolate vermicelli.

Makes about 12

Macaroons

25 g (1 oz) whole almonds, blanched
100 g (4 oz) ground almonds
225 g (8 oz) caster sugar
2 large egg whites, whisked
15 g ($\frac{1}{2}$ oz) ground rice
3 ml ($\frac{1}{2}$ teaspoon) almond essence

Split the whole blanched almonds in halves. Put the ground almonds, sugar and egg whites in a bowl and mix them together, then add the ground rice and almond essence. Put the mixture into a piping bag fitted with 1·25-cm ($\frac{1}{2}$-in) plain pipe. Pipe small rounds on to non-stick paper on baking trays, leaving plenty of room for the macaroons to spread. Top each one with a split almond. Bake them at 180°C (350°F)/Gas 4 for about 20 minutes. Cool on a wire rack.

Makes about 24

Gingernuts

75 g (3 oz) margarine
175 g (6 oz) Demerara sugar
250 g (9 oz) plain flour
pinch of salt
5 ml (1 level teaspoon) bicarbonate of soda
10 ml (2 level teaspoons) ground ginger
5 ml (1 level teaspoon) ground mixed spice
pinch of ground nutmeg
60 ml (4 tablespoons) golden syrup

Cream the margarine and sugar together until light and fluffy. Sift in the flour, salt, bicarbonate of soda, ginger, mixed spice and nutmeg. Mix well with a wooden spoon, adding the golden syrup to give a stiff dough. Form the mixture into 2·5-cm (1-in) balls in the palms of your hands, then flatten them on greased trays, allowing plenty of room for spreading. Bake at 190°C (375°F)/Gas 5 for about 15 minutes.

Makes about 36

Ginger Flapjacks

175 g (6 oz) butter	225 g (8 oz) porridge oats
100 g (4 oz) Demerara sugar	5 ml (1 level teaspoon) ground ginger
25 g (1 oz) golden syrup	

Put the butter, sugar and golden syrup in a large pan and heat gently until the sugar has melted. Stir in the oats and the ground ginger and mix well. Press the mixture into a greased Swiss roll tin and smooth the surface. Bake it at 150°C (300°F)/Gas 2 for about 45 minutes or until it is a rich golden brown. Cut into fingers when it has cooled a little and lift when it is completely cold.

Makes about 18

Brandy Snaps

50 g (2 oz) granulated sugar	pinch of salt
30 ml (2 tablespoons) golden syrup	10 ml (2 level teaspoons) ground ginger
50 g (2 oz) butter	15 ml (1 tablespoon) lemon juice, strained
50 g (2 oz) plain flour	

Put the sugar, syrup and butter into a saucepan and heat gently until the sugar has dissolved. Sift the flour, salt and ginger together and stir them into the melted ingredients with the lemon juice. Mix well. Drop teaspoons of the mixture on to greased baking trays, 4 to a tray and at least 10 cm (4 in) apart to allow for spreading. Bake them, one tray at a time, at 180°C (350°F)/Gas 4 for about 10 minutes. When they come out of the oven, allow to cool a little, remove each one with a palette knife and roll it round a greased wooden spoon handle. Put on to wire racks to cool. If at any time some do become too brittle to roll, put the tray back in the oven for a couple of minutes.

Makes about 10

Shortbread

75 g (3 oz) unsalted butter, softened
75 g (3 oz) plain flour, sifted

25 g (1 oz) rice flour
40 g (1½ oz) caster sugar
25 g (1 oz) ground almonds

Crumble the butter into the flour until the mixture looks like fine breadcrumbs, adding the rice flour as and when the mixture becomes sticky. You might not need all of the rice flour. Stir in the sugar and ground almonds and put the mixture in a 15-cm (6-in) sandwich tin and smooth the top. Grainy pieces will disappear during the cooking so don't work this mixture too much. Make a pattern on the top and prick the centre with a fork. Bake at 150°C (300°F)/Gas 2 for about 1 hour or until the shortbread is a very pale biscuit colour. Leave to cool in the tin but cut it into neat wedges before it is completely cold.

Makes 8 wedges

Coconut Crisps

225 g (8 oz) self-raising
   flour
pinch of salt
125 g (5 oz) butter
100 g (4 oz) caster sugar

50 g (2 oz) desiccated
   coconut
few drops vanilla essence
1 large egg, beaten

Sift the flour with the salt. Cream the butter and sugar together until light and fluffy. Stir in the coconut, vanilla essence, egg and flour and mix to a stiff dough with your hands. Knead on a lightly-floured board until the mixture is smooth. Roll the dough thinly and cut it into about 36 rounds using a 7-cm (3-in) plain cutter. Place the biscuits on greased baking trays and bake them at 180°C (350°F)/ Gas 4 for 12–15 minutes. Cool for a couple of minutes on the baking trays, then transfer to wire racks to finish cooling.

Makes about 36

Shrewsbury Biscuits

100 g (4 oz) butter
125 g (5 oz) caster sugar
1 large egg, beaten

225 g (8 oz) plain flour,
   sifted

Cream the butter and 100 g (4 oz) sugar until it is soft and fluffy, then beat in the egg and the flour. Mix to a smooth dough. Knead it on a lightly-floured board, then roll the dough thinly and cut it into rounds using a 6-cm (2½-in) fluted cutter. Place the biscuits on greased baking trays and bake them at 180°C (350°F)/Gas 4 for 12–15 minutes until they are just coloured golden. Allow to cool for 2 minutes on the baking trays, sprinkling with the rest of the sugar, then transfer them to wire racks to finish cooling.

Makes about 36

Florentines

100 g (4 oz) butter
100 g (4 oz) caster sugar
100 g (4 oz) walnuts and
  almonds, mixed and
  chopped
50 g (2 oz) glacé cherries,
  chopped

50 g (2 oz) chopped mixed
  peel
50 g (2 oz) sultanas
15 ml (1 tablespoon)
  double cream
100 g (4 oz) plain
  chocolate, melted

Melt the butter and add the sugar and when the sugar has dissolved, boil the mixture for 1 minute. Stir in the nuts, cherries, peel and sultanas. Stir in the cream and mix well. Drop the mixture in small heaps on baking trays lined with non-stick paper. Allow plenty of room for spreading. Bake at 180°C (350°F)/Gas 4 for about 10 minutes until golden brown. Remove from the oven, one tray at a time, and neaten the edges of each biscuit with a knife blade. When they have cooled a little on the trays and are beginning to become firm, use a palette knife to transfer them to cooling racks. Finish by spreading the melted chocolate on the flat backs of the Florentines with a knife, then marking the chocolate into lines with the back of a fork.

Makes about 12

Coconut Ice

0·5 kg (1 lb) granulated
  sugar
60 ml (4 tablespoons) milk

125 g (5 oz) desiccated
  coconut
cochineal

Put the sugar, milk and 60 ml (4 tablespoons) cold water into a large saucepan and heat very gently to dissolve the sugar. Bring to the boil and boil for 10–12 minutes until the temperature reaches 116°C (240°F) or forms a soft ball when a little is dropped into a cup of cold water. Remove the pan from the heat while you do this test. As soon as it's ready, remove from the heat and stir in the coconut. Quickly pour half the mixture into a greased 15-cm (6-in) square cake tin. Colour the remainder pink with a few drops of cochineal and spread it swiftly over the white layer. You must do this quickly; otherwise the two layers tend to separate. Mark into 2·5-cm (1-in) squares when half set, and break when completely cold.

Makes about 36 pieces

Peppermint Creams

0·5 kg (1 lb) icing sugar, sifted
5 ml (1 teaspoon) glycerine

2 egg whites, beaten
oil of peppermint
green vegetable colouring

Put the icing sugar in a large bowl and mix in the glycerine and egg whites until you have a firm consistency. Knead to make the mixture smooth. Knead in a few drops of peppermint oil and green vegetable colouring, then roll the mixture to a 0·5-cm ($\frac{1}{4}$-in) thickness on a working surface lightly dusted with icing sugar. Cut out 2·5-cm (1-in) rounds with a small plain cutter and leave them on baking trays to harden.

Makes about 40

Chocolate Nutties

100 g (4 oz) blanched hazelnuts, chopped
450 g (1 lb) plain chocolate, melted

25 g (1 oz) butter
4 large egg yolks
100 g (4 oz) chopped mixed nuts, toasted

Stir the hazelnuts into the chocolate and when the mixture has slightly cooled, stir in the butter and egg yolks. Replace the mixture over hot water and stir it for a couple of minutes. Leave to cool, then roll the mixture into 30 small balls. Roll these in the toasted nuts and leave to set.

Makes about 30

Honeycomb Toffee

450 g (1 lb) granulated
  sugar
pinch of cream of tartar

30 ml (2 tablespoons)
  golden syrup
5 ml (1 level teaspoon)
  bicarbonate of soda

Put the sugar, cream of tartar and golden syrup in a large saucepan and add 125 ml ($\frac{1}{4}$ pint) cold water. Heat gently to dissolve the sugar, then bring to the boil and boil until the temperature reaches 149°C (300°F) or when a little of the syrup forms brittle threads when dropped into a jug of water. Remove from the heat. Blend the bicarbonate of soda with 10 ml (1 dessertspoon) cold water and add it to the toffee, stirring well. Pour it quickly into a greased 18-cm. (7-in) tin and leave it to set. Just before it sets completely mark it into squares with a sharp knife and leave until cold, Break into pieces when set.

Makes about 49 pieces

Peanut Brittle

400 g (14 oz) granulated
  sugar
150 g (6 oz) soft brown
  sugar
150 g (6 oz) golden syrup

50 g (2 oz) butter
2 ml ($\frac{1}{4}$ teaspoon)
  bicarbonate of soda
300 g (12 oz) unsalted
  peanuts, chopped

Put the granulated and brown sugar with the golden syrup and 125 ml (¼ pint) cold water in a large pan and heat gently until the sugars have dissolved. Add the butter, bring to the boil and boil until the temperature reaches 149°C (300°F) or a little of the syrup forms brittle threads when dropped into cold water. Add the bicarbonate of soda and the nuts and pour the mixture into a greased 20-cm (8-in) square tin. Just before it completely sets, mark into squares and leave to cool completely.

Makes about 64 pieces

Toffee Apples

1 kg (2 lb) Demerara sugar
100 g (4 oz) butter
20 ml (4 teaspoons) vinegar
30 ml (2 tablespoons)
  golden syrup

15 medium-sized eating
  apples
15 wooden sticks

Put the sugar, butter, vinegar and golden syrup in a large pan with 250 ml (½ pint) cold water. Heat gently until the sugar has dissolved, then bring to the boil and boil until the

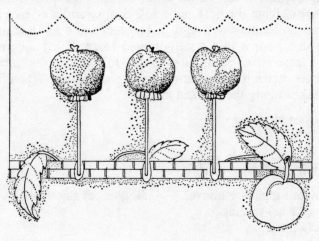

temperature reaches 143°C (290°F). Wipe the apples and push the wooden sticks securely into the cores. Dip each apple into the toffee, twirl it around for a couple of seconds and put to cool and harden on non-stick paper on baking trays. Wrap each toffee apple in waxed paper, twisting it around the stick to hold it securely.

Makes 15

Vanilla Fudge

0·5 kg (1 lb) granulated
   sugar
50 g (2 oz) butter

125 ml (¼ pint) evaporated
   milk
125 ml (¼ pint) milk
vanilla essence

Put the sugar, butter, evaporated milk and ordinary milk in a large saucepan and heat gently until the sugar dissolves. Bring to the boil and boil gently, stirring occasionally, until the syrup reaches 116°C (240°F). Another way to test this is to drop some of the syrup into a bowl of cold water; if it forms a soft ball when you squeeze it between your fingers, it's ready. Take the pan off the heat if you are testing it this way because it will go on to the toffee stage quite quickly. Remove from the heat and add 3 drops vanilla essence and beat the mixture well until it becomes thick and grainy in texture. Pour it into a well-greased 15-cm (6-in) square tin and leave it for 30 minutes to set. Just before it sets completely, mark it into squares with a sharp knife. When firm, break it along the marked lines.

Makes 36 pieces

Fruit and Nut Fudge

vanilla fudge (see above)
50 g (2 oz) walnuts,
   chopped

50 g (2 oz) sultanas

Make the vanilla fudge and when you remove it from the heat, stir in the walnuts and sultanas and beat until the mixture is thick and grainy. Pour it into a greased 18-cm (7-in) square tin and allow to set, marking it into squares just before setting.

Makes 49 pieces

Chocolate Fudge

0·5 kg (1 lb) caster sugar   100 g (4 oz) butter
125 ml (¼ pint) double   100 g (4 oz) plain
    cream   chocolate, grated

Put the sugar, cream, butter and chocolate in a large pan and follow the method given for vanilla fudge (see page 124). Pour it into a 15-cm (6-in) square tin and leave to set, marking it into squares before it sets completely.

Makes 36 pieces

Drinks

Although there isn't a closed season for drinking, the summer months provide all the best opportunities for making pretty concoctions in frosted jugs. Long cooling drinks made with or without alcohol give you plenty of choice, and for the children there are ice cream sodas, milk shakes, orange drinks and ginger beer, though home-made ginger beer can be very potent with a high alcohol content.

Summer fruits may be mashed to a purée and used as a base for drinks or added whole as decoration and delicate flavouring. If you've got a herb garden, this is your chance to experiment with lovage, borage, lemon thyme, lemon balm and the many varieties of mint such as pineapple, spearmint and ginger.

Cherry Ripe

75 g (3 oz) caster sugar
225 g (8 oz) ripe Morello
 cherries, stoned
2 bottles sparkling rosé
 wine, chilled

60 ml (4 tablespoons)
 cherry brandy
2 small bottles soda water

Put the sugar in a small pan with the cherries and 125 ml
($\frac{1}{4}$ pint) cold water. Heat gently to dissolve the sugar, then
bring to the boil and boil for 3 minutes or until the cherries
are soft but not breaking. Allow to chill in the fridge. Stir
the cherries and their syrup into the rosé with the cherry
brandy. Just on the point of serving, add the soda water.

Serves 10–12

Apricot Fizzer

0·5 kg (1 lb) ripe apricots,
 stoned
1 wine glass vodka

1 bottle sparkling white
 wine, chilled

Use only very ripe apricots for this drink and push them
through a sieve to make a purée. Stir in the vodka and chill
in the fridge. Chill the wine at the same time. When ready
to serve, pour in the wine, stir briskly and pour into glasses.

Serves 8

Ginger Beer

Ginger beer plant:
50 g (2 oz) fresh yeast
10 ml (1 level dessertspoon)
 caster sugar
30 ml (2 level tablespoons)
 ground ginger

Additions:
50 ml (10 level teaspoons)
 ground ginger
550 g ($1\frac{1}{4}$ lb) caster sugar
juice of 2 large lemons,
 strained

Cream the yeast with the caster sugar until it is liquid. Stir in the ground ginger and 250 ml ($\frac{1}{2}$ pint) cold water. Mix well and pour it into a large jar with a covering of two layers of muslin secured with an elastic band. Every day for 10 days, stir in 5 ml (1 level teaspoon) ground ginger and 5 ml (1 level teaspoon) caster sugar.

Dissolve the remaining sugar in 1 litre ($1\frac{3}{4}$ pints) water, bring to the boil and allow to cool to lukewarm. Stir in the lemon juice. Strain the ginger beer plant through its muslin covering into the sugar and lemon juice mixture. Stir in 3 litres (5 pints) water. Stir well and bottle at once in strong, very clean screw-topped cider or beer bottles. Store in a cool place, and not somewhere which tends to get warm during the day or your ginger beer will burst and fizz all over the place.

When you want to make more ginger beer, halve the ginger beer plant (all that's left in the jar after straining) and put it in another jam jar. Add 250 ml ($\frac{1}{2}$ pint) water to the jar and 10 ml (2 level teaspoons) each of ground ginger and caster sugar, then continue as above, adding to the jar each day for ten days and completing with the lemon juice and extra sugar.

Makes about 4·5 litres (1 gallon)

Sangria

$\frac{1}{2}$ large orange, sliced	1 bottle dry red Spanish
1 large lemon, sliced	wine
$\frac{1}{2}$ large eating apple, thinly sliced	60 ml (4 tablespoons) brandy
75 g (3 oz) caster sugar	1 large bottle soda water
	sprigs of mint

Put the fruit slices, sugar, wine and brandy into a very large jug and stir well. Chill in the fridge for at least 1 hour. Chill the soda water separately. Just before serving, add the soda

water and pour into chilled glasses. Garnish if liked with
mint sprigs.

Serves 8

Kir

1 wine glass crème de cassis   4 wine glasses dry white
                                   wine

Chill both the crème de cassis and the wine before pouring
the cassis into 4 glasses. Pour on the wine, stir and serve
at once.

Serves 4

Caribbean Shake

60 ml (4 level tablespoons)   750 ml (1½ pints) milk
   drinking chocolate   483-ml (17-oz) block vanilla
15 ml (1 level tablespoon)   ice cream
   instant coffee   15 ml (1 tablespoon) tia
45 ml (3 tablespoons)   maria
   boiling water   ground cinnamon

Dissolve the chocolate and instant coffee in the boiling water
and leave it to cool. Pour the milk into a blender, add the
coffee liquid and the ice cream and blend until frothy. Stir
in the tia maria and pour into tall glasses. Sprinkle with the
cinnamon to serve.

Serves 4

Wedding Special

0·5 kg (1 lb) raspberries
12 mint sprigs
100 g (4 oz) caster sugar
½ bottle brandy

1 bottle sparkling rosé wine
3 bottles sparkling dry
    white wine
rose petals

Wash the raspberries and remove the stalks and cores. Only use the very best berries for this wine cup. Wash the mint sprigs and put them with the raspberries in the serving bowl. Sprinkle with the sugar, pour on the brandy and leave to stand for 1 hour. Chill the wines, then pour them on the raspberry mixture. To serve, float the well-washed rose petals on the punch.

Serves 20–25

Sunshine Stinger

¼ bottle vodka
1 medium-sized orange,
   sliced
1 small grapefruit, sliced

2 litres (3½ pints) white
   wine, chilled
2 litres (3½ pints) ginger
   beer, chilled

Put the vodka with the orange and grapefruit slices (including the peel) into a jug and leave them overnight to soak. Next day, pour on the chilled white wine. Make sure the ginger beer is also chilled and add this just before serving.

Serves 20–25

Cider Apple Cup

4 red eating apples, sliced
1 large lemon, thinly sliced
2·5-cm (1-in) piece
   cucumber, thinly sliced
12 whole cloves
25 g (1 oz) caster sugar

125 ml (¼ pint) boiling
   water
1 litre (1¾ pints) dry cider,
   chilled
1 large bottle soda water,
   chilled

Put the apple, lemon and cucumber slices in a large jug with the whole cloves. Put the sugar and boiling water in a small pan, heat gently until the sugar has dissolved, then boil until the mixture is syrupy. Pour on to the fruit and leave in the fridge to chill. Stir in the cider and soda water just before serving.

Serves 6–8

Irish Coffee

30 ml (2 level tablespoons)
    ground coffee
500 ml (1 pint) boiling
    water
20 ml (4 level teaspoons)
    caster sugar

120 ml (8 tablespoons)
    Irish whiskey
142-g (5-oz) carton double
    cream

Put the ground coffee in a jug, pour on the freshly boiling water, stir well and leave to infuse for 5 minutes. Rinse 4 stemmed glasses with hot water and strain in the coffee to within 1·75 cm (¾ in) of the top of the glass. Stir in the sugar and pour in the whiskey. Gently add the cream by holding the tip of a spoon at the surface of the coffee and the edge of the glass, with the back uppermost, and pouring the cream on to the back of the spoon. The cream should sit in an unbroken layer across the top of the coffee. Serve at once.

Serves 4

Strawberry Milk Shake

500 ml (1 pint) milk,
    chilled
100 g (4 oz) ripe
    strawberries, hulled

30 ml (2 tablespoons)
    strawberry milk shake
    syrup
120 ml (8 tablespoons)
    strawberry ice cream

Pour the milk into a large blender goblet, add the strawberries, milk-shake syrup and ice cream and blend until the mixture is frothy and smooth. Serve in tall glasses with straws.

Serves 4–6

Turkish Coffee

75 g (3 oz) very finely
  ground coffee

75 g (3 oz) caster sugar
few drops rose water

Put the coffee, sugar and 500 ml (1 pint) cold water into a very small saucepan. Stir it over a medium heat until the mixture comes to the boil and becomes frothy. Remove from the heat, and when the froth has subsided return the pan to the heat and stir it again until it boils.

Just before serving, add 15 ml (1 tablespoon) cold water to settle the grounds and add a few drops of rose water. Pour the coffee into small cups and serve Turkish style with a glass of water for each person. Never add milk to Turkish coffee, although you can make it with more or less sugar than is suggested here.

Serves 4

Iced Coffee

50 g (2 oz) finely ground
  coffee
caster sugar
ice cubes

142-g (5-oz) carton
  double cream, whipped
ground nutmeg

Put the coffee in a small pan with 1 litre (1¾ pints) cold water and bring it to the boil very slowly. Remove from the heat and allow it to stand, stirring it occasionally, for 5 minutes. Strain into a jug and while it is still hot add sugar to taste. Stir until the sugar has dissolved, then chill the coffee in the fridge. To serve, pour into chilled glasses, add a few ice cubes, top with a dollop of softly-whipped cream and sprinkle with a little ground nutmeg.

Serves 6

Fruit Crush

2 large bottles apple juice
250 ml (½ pint) soda water
100 g (4 oz) granulated
  sugar
2·5-cm (1-in) stick of
  cinnamon
1 large lemon

1 large orange, thinly
  sliced
2·5-cm (1-in) piece
  cucumber, thinly sliced
50 g (2 oz) strawberries,
  hulled
50 g (2 oz) white grapes

Chill the apple juice and soda water in the fridge, separately, for at least 2 hours. Put the sugar with 125 ml (¼ pint) cold water in a pan. Heat gently until the sugar has dissolved, then boil for 1 minute. Remove from the heat and add the cinnamon stick. Wash and thinly peel the lemon rind and add it to the syrup. Leave to cool.

Squeeze out and strain the lemon juice and pour it into a large jug with the apple juice and soda water. Add the orange slices and cucumber. Halve the strawberries and the grapes and remove the grape pips. Add both to the jug. Strain in the cold sugar syrup and serve chilled.

Serves 8

Minty Cooler

1 large lemon
125 ml (¼ pint) lime juice
  cordial
ice cubes

2·5-cm (1-in) piece
  cucumber, thinly sliced
sprigs of mint

Finely peel off the lemon rind, leaving the pith on the lemon. Put the peel in a jug. Squeeze out and strain the lemon juice and add to the jug with the lime juice cordial and the ice cubes. Pour in 1 litre (1¾ pints) cold water and leave to chill in the fridge for 2 hours. Just before serving, add the cucumber slices and mint sprigs and serve at once.

Serves 8

Raspberry Ice Cream Soda

120 ml (8 tablespoons)   1 bottle cream soda
  raspberry ripple ice cream   raspberry milk shake syrup

Scoop the ice cream into 4 tall glasses and top up with the cream soda. Drizzle a little milk-shake syrup over the ice cream when it comes to the surface and serve with straws and a long spoon.

Serves 4

Orangeade

3 large oranges   75 g (3 oz) caster sugar
1 large lemon   500 ml (1 pint) boiling water

Wash the fruit and thinly pare off the rinds, leaving all the white and bitter pith on the fruit. Squeeze out and strain the fruit juices. Put the rinds, sugar and boiling water in a bowl and leave to cool, stirring occasionally. Finally add the fruit juices, strain the orangeade into a jug and serve.

All citrus fruits can be made into a refreshing drink in this way. Lemon is particularly good.

Serves 8

Iced Orange Tea

15 ml (1 level tablespoon)   2 large oranges
  China tea   ice cubes
500 ml (1 pint) boiling   single white blossoms,
  water   well washed
25 g (1 oz) caster sugar

Put the tea in a large jug, pour on the boiling water and stir in the sugar. Leave the tea to infuse for 5 minutes, then strain it through a nylon strainer into another jug. Peel off the orange rind, without removing any of the pith from the oranges. Squeeze out and strain the juice. Add peel and juice to the tea and leave it in the fridge for 2–4 hours to chill. Remove the rind and add ice cubes to serve. Float the flowers in the jug on the orange tea.

Serves 4

Mint Tea

12 sprigs of mint, washed   50 g (2 oz) caster sugar

Crush the mint sprigs and put them in a pan with 500 ml (1 pint) water. Bring slowly to the boil, then leave the mixture for 10 minutes to infuse. Stir in the caster sugar. Strain the mixture into a jug and leave it in the fridge to chill. Serve in small glasses.

Serves 4–6

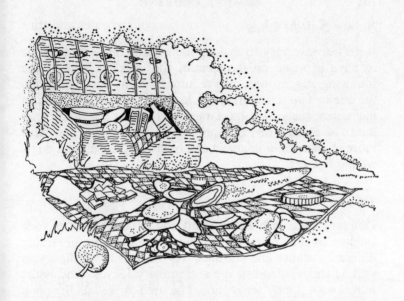

Picnics and Barbecues

This is a chapter with suggestions for outdoor eating, whether it's an impromptu picnic, a cricket tea, lunch in the garden or a barbecue. Cooking out of doors is a good occupation and a more relaxed one than producing the same meal in the kitchen. And because everyone seems to get involved in the preparation, it's much more of a family undertaking than is usual with cooking. Often it's the men who do the work, so here are plenty of different recipes to satisfy even the most ardent barbecue man. But it's the great British invention, the sandwich, which will always be the most convenient, favourite and easy answer to 'What shall we take with us?' so this chapter begins with a variety of ways to make your sandwiches really tasty.

137

Super Sandwiches

It isn't always easy to make good sandwiches if you decide to have a picnic on the spur of the moment. But of the following suggestions, you're sure to have the ingredients for one or two in the fridge or larder. If you're called on to make sandwiches for bazaars, fêtes, cricket teas and other kinds of event when outdoor eating is planned, you have more chance to think ahead and organise yourself and a few willing helpers.

Bread

Different kinds of bread not only add to the flavours of your sandwiches but help when arranging a table by providing different colours and textures. Try brown, the ordinary as well as the wholemeal, rye and granary loaves. And white loaves with poppy seeds should be used as well as the plain sandwich loaf. Cut loaves save time, and you'll find about 24 thin slices in a large packet. Cut the same size loaf yourself and you'll probably manage about 20. It's important to use really fresh bread, especially when you're making rolled sandwiches.

Butter

Soften the butter so that it's easy to spread or use one of the soft margarines, spreading right to the crusts unless you're going to cut them off. Allow 175 g (6 oz) for a large loaf. Making your own savoury butters adds to the interest and often saves time, and you'll find a few suggestions for these at the end of the fillings.

Fillings

Well-flavoured fillings combat the effect of a double casing of bread and butter. They should be moist but not to the point of wetting the bread. Therefore it's worth remembering to put a layer of lettuce between tomato fillings and the bread, or to spread a slightly thicker layer of butter to prevent extra moist fillings from making soggy sandwiches.

1. Mash canned salmon and mix it with plenty of pepper and a little salt, mayonnaise and chopped cucumber.
2. Mince cooked chicken and stir in some mayonnaise or sandwich spread.
3. Chop hard-boiled eggs and add some finely chopped onion, parsley, chives or thyme and a little mayonnaise.
4. Cream some soft cheese with finely chopped pineapple and a few toasted chopped nuts. Curd, cream and cottage cheeses are good like this.
5. Mash some canned tuna and mix it with a few drops of vinegar, plenty of salt and pepper, chopped watercress and a little sandwich spread.
6. Mince the last of the cold roast beef and mix it with creamed horseradish sauce, adding a little salad cream if it's too hot.
7. Stir a little lemon juice into mashed sardines, add some chopped onion and cucumber and season well.
8. Grate Cheddar or a similar hard cheese or a blue cheese and mix it with mayonnaise or salad cream.
9. Grate an apple and mix with it some lemon juice, honey and a few chopped hazelnuts.
10. Mix canned or fresh crab meat with a little double cream, a few drops of vinegar, plenty of salt and pepper and some chopped celery, green pepper, cucumber or tomato.
11. Scramble some eggs and mix with a little crisply fried bacon and some salad cream.

The following flavoured butters are particularly useful for rolled sandwiches when the filling must not be bulky:
12. Finely chop some cooked tongue and mix it with softened butter. Add a pinch or two of curry powder and some finely chopped onion.
13. Mash 4 anchovy fillets to a paste with some butter and season with chopped parsley and paprika.
14. Stir some tomato paste into softened butter, season well and use with a plain filling of cucumber or lettuce.

15. Parsley, thyme, basil or marjoram may be chopped and beaten into a softened butter.

Garlic Bread

1 long French loaf	1 clove garlic, crushed
100 g (4 oz) butter, softened	

Cut the loaf into 2·5-cm (1-in) slices diagonally to the bottom crust but not through it. All the slices should be joined along the bottom of the loaf. Put the bread on a large piece of foil. Beat the butter with the garlic until it is really soft, then spread it in the cuts on both sides of the slices. Wrap the foil round the loaf to seal it and place it on a baking tray. Put the baking tray on the barbecue or if there's little room put the parcel straight on the grids and leave for 10–15 minutes until it is hot and crisp, turning it occasionally. If you make it in the oven bake it at 200°C (400°F)/Gas 6 for about 20 minutes. Serve hot straight from the foil.

Serves 6–8

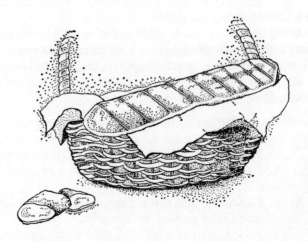

Cheesy Herb Bread

1 long French loaf,
   prepared
150 g (6 oz) soft cream
   cheese
salt and pepper

5 ml (1 level teaspoon)
   chives, chopped
5 ml (1 level teaspoon)
   lemon thyme, chopped
10 ml (2 level teaspoons)
   parsley, finely chopped

Prepare the loaf as you would for garlic bread. Beat the cream cheese in a bowl until it is very soft and season it with salt and pepper. Beat in the chives, lemon thyme and parsley and spread this mixture in the cuts on both sides of the bread slices. Wrap the loaf in foil and bake it on a hot barbecue for 10–15 minutes or in the oven at 200°C (400°F)/Gas 6 for about 20 minutes. Serve from the foil parcel.

Serves 6–8

Sausagemeat Patties

1 kg (2 lb) pork
   sausagemeat
1 large onion, chopped
salt and pepper
10 ml (2 level teaspoons)
   sage, finely chopped

5 ml (1 level teaspoon)
   parsley, finely chopped
1 large egg, beaten
30 ml (2 tablespoons)
   cooking oil
10 soft hamburger buns
brown sauce

Break the sausagemeat up with a fork and mix in the onion, salt and pepper, sage, parsley and egg. Form the mixture into 10 flat cakes. Lay them on the grid of a barbecue, brush them with a little oil and cook them until they turn dark brown on both sides. Split each bun, fill with a patty and add a dollop of brown sauce.

Serves 10

Spicy Bananas

6 large bananas, peeled
60 ml (4 tablespoons)
   honey

10 ml (2 level teaspoons)
   ground cinnamon
25 g (1 oz) chopped nuts

Put the bananas on a large piece of foil. Spoon on the honey and the cinnamon, mix well and wrap the foil into a baggy parcel to seal it. Put it on the barbecue and bake it for 5–10 minutes, shaking it often to turn the bananas and mix them with the spiced honey. Unwrap the parcel, sprinkle the bananas with the nuts and serve hot.

Serves 6

Hamburgers

1 small onion, finely
   chopped
1 large egg, beaten
325 g (12 oz) raw minced
   beef
salt and pepper

30 ml (2 tablespoons)
   cooking oil
4 lettuce leaves, prepared
2 large tomatoes, sliced
45 ml (3 tablespoons)
   mayonnaise (see page 40)
4 large soft rolls, halved

Mix the onion, beaten egg and beef together and season the mixture well with salt and pepper. Form it into 4 hamburgers. Cook them for about 7 minutes on a hot barbecue grill, turning them once or twice and brushing them often with the oil.

Sandwich one hamburger with some lettuce and tomato slices and a little mayonnaise between one soft roll. Complete the other hamburgers in the same way. Wrap each one in a napkin to serve.

Makes 4

Lamb Kebabs

4 small onions, skinned
1 small green pepper,
  prepared
4 small tomatoes
0·5 kg (1 lb) lean shoulder
  of lamb, cubed
8 bay leaves
100 g (4 oz) button
  mushrooms
salt and pepper
60 ml (4 tablespoons)
  cooking oil

If the onions are large, cut them in half along the horizontal (if you cut them from stem to root you'll have difficulty putting them on the skewer). Cut the green pepper into large squares. Halve the tomatoes, again along the horizontal, if they are large. Divide the ingredients into 8 portions and thread them on to 8 skewers, alternating the meat with the vegetables, bay leaves and mushrooms. Season them with salt and pepper and brush them with a little of the oil. Lay them on a hot barbecue grill and cook them for about 15 minutes, until they are tender and the vegetables are just beginning to singe at the edges. Brush them with a little more oil each time you turn them. Serve with one of the barbecue sauces.

Serves 8

Lamb Tikka Kebabs

0·75 kg (1½ lb) lean shoulder
  of lamb
142-g (5-oz) carton plain
  yoghurt
2 ml (¼ teaspoon) ground
  coriander
2 ml (¼ teaspoon) ground
  cumin
5 ml (1 level teaspoon)
  hot chilli, finely chopped
1 clove garlic, crushed
5-cm (2-in) piece green
  root ginger, peeled
salt
1 large lemon
pepper

Cut the lamb into 2·5-cm (1-in) cubes, discarding any fat and gristle. Whisk the yoghurt with the coriander, cumin, chilli and garlic. Finely chop the ginger and add to the yoghurt with a good pinch of salt. Cut the lemon in half and squeeze out and strain the juice from one half. Add to the yoghurt. Stir this sauce into the pieces of lamb and leave them to marinate for 1 hour, stirring them frequently.

Remove the lamb from the marinade, thread it on to skewers and grill them over a hot fire, turning them frequently and brushing them during the 5 minutes' cooking with some of the marinade. Sprinkle with pepper and serve the skewers with thin slices cut from the remaining lemon half. Finely shredded lettuce is all that's needed to go with this dish for summer eating.

Serves 6

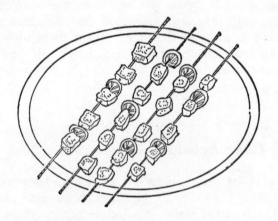

Pineapple Barbecue Sauce

2 large onions, finely
    chopped
25 g (1 oz) butter
125 ml (¼ pint) tomato
    juice

250 ml (½ pint) pineapple
    juice
Worcestershire sauce
salt and pepper

Fry the onions in the butter until they are golden and soft. Pour in the tomato and pineapple juices, season with a few drops of Worcestershire sauce until it tastes spicy, and then add salt and pepper. Transfer the sauce to the barbecue and let it simmer towards the edge while you cook meats in the centre. Either pour it over cooked foods, or let people dip their portions in as they eat.

Serves 4–8

Redhot Sauce

120 ml (8 level
 tablespoons) redcurrant
 jelly
5 ml (1 level teaspoon)
 mustard powder
5 ml (1 teaspoon) tabasco
 sauce
25 g (1 oz) butter

salt and pepper
10 ml (1 dessertspoon)
 lemon juice, strained
60 ml (4 tablespoons)
 tomato paste
60 ml (4 tablespoons)
 vinegar

Combine all the ingredients, stir them well, stand the pan at the edge of the barbecue and let it simmer while you cook other things. Dip cooked meats and vegetables into this sauce or spoon it over.

Serves 4–8

Barbecue Daubing Sauce

250 ml (½ pint) vinegar
30 ml (2 tablespoons)
 Worcestershire sauce
75 g (3 oz) brown sugar

60 ml (4 tablespoons)
 tomato ketchup
100 g (4 oz) butter, melted

Mix all the ingredients in a pan and heat them gently until

the sugar has melted, then stir them well and keep the sauce simmering at the side of the barbecue. Use this to paint on to all raw meats before you grill them on the barbecue.

Barbecue Baked Fruits

4 small cooking apples,
  cored
4 hard pears, cored
100 g (4 oz) sultanas
60 ml (4 tablespoons) honey

15 ml (1 tablespoon) lemon
  juice, strained
50 g (2 oz) dried apricots,
  finely chopped

Use a corer and prepare the apples and pears the same way. Make a cut through the skin around the middle of the fruits, so that they won't burst during cooking. Mix the sultanas, honey, lemon juice and apricots in a bowl and, using a spoon, stuff this mixture into the cores. Wrap each fruit in foil, sealing it at the top by twisting it. Stand the fruits at the edge of the barbecue for a good hour and check to see if they are done by squeezing them through the foil. Pears usually cook a little faster than apples.

Serves 8

Mushroom Cream Soup

225 g (8 oz) mushrooms,
  sliced
1 medium-sized onion,
  finely chopped
250 ml (½ pint) good
  chicken stock

25 g (1 oz) butter
25 g (1 oz) plain flour
375 ml (¾ pint) milk
125 ml (¼ pint) single
  cream
salt and pepper

Put the mushrooms, onion and stock in a large pan and bring to the boil. Cover and simmer for 40 minutes, then blend in an electric blender. Melt the butter in the rinsed pan, stir in the flour and cook the mixture for 1 minute. Gradually mix in the blended mushrooms and milk and bring to the boil, stirring all the time. Reduce the heat and simmer the soup for 20 minutes. Stir in the cream and season with salt and pepper.

You can serve this soup just warm, or chilled, for hot days. If you want to keep it hot on the barbecue, stand it towards the back in a cooler spot.

Serves 8

Guacamole

2 large very ripe avocados	1 small onion, grated
salt and pepper	1 clove garlic, crushed
juice of 1 lemon, strained	chilli pepper

Using a stainless steel knife, peel the avocados, cut them in half, remove the stones and mash the flesh to a smooth purée. Season quickly with salt and pepper and stir in the lemon juice to prevent the purée from turning brown. Mix in the onion and garlic and season with plenty of chilli pepper. Serve with crusty French bread as a dip.

Serves 8

Sweet and Sour Chicken Drumsticks

8 large chicken drumsticks	75 g (3 oz) brown sugar
salt and pepper	5 ml (1 teaspoon) tabasco sauce
	1 clove garlic, crushed
Sweet and sour sauce:	salt and pepper
90 ml (6 tablespoons) soy sauce	125 ml ($\frac{1}{4}$ pint) vinegar
90 ml (6 tablespoons) tomato ketchup	125 ml ($\frac{1}{4}$ pint) pineapple juice

Wipe the chicken drumsticks and season them with salt and pepper. Put them on the barbecue and grill them slowly for 10–15 minutes until they are crisply browned on all sides, turning them often.

Mix all the ingredients for the sweet and sour sauce and heat it gently in a foil dish large enough to hold the chicken drumsticks. Make sure the sugar has dissolved before you put the chicken into the sauce. Add the drumsticks, spoon the sauce all over them and let them sit at the side of the barbecue for 15 minutes before serving them.

Serves 8

Corn and Mushroom Quiche

shortcrust pastry (see page 67)
25 g (1 oz) butter
100 g (4 oz) mushrooms, sliced
225 g (8 oz) sweetcorn kernels (see page 13)
3 large eggs, beaten
125 ml ($\frac{1}{4}$ pint) single cream
125 ml ($\frac{1}{4}$ pint) milk
salt and pepper

Make the shortcrust pastry and use it to line a 25-cm (10-in) flan dish. Trim the edge.

Melt the butter in a pan and fry the mushrooms for 5 minutes, stirring them all the time. Mix with the sweetcorn and scatter all over the flan. Beat the eggs with the cream and milk, season very well and pour this mixture into the flan. Bake at 190°C (375°F)/Gas 5 for 30 minutes or until it is golden brown and well risen. Allow to cool before wrapping it for a picnic.

Serves 8–10

Cold Sausage Salad

0·5 kg (1 lb) good
  sausages
225 g (8 oz) red beans,
  cooked
1 large onion, roughly
  chopped
1 green pepper, roughly
  chopped

100 g (4 oz) sweetcorn
  kernels (see page 13)
vinaigrette (see page 16)
15 ml (1 level tablespoon)
  parsley, roughly chopped
30 ml (2 level tablespoons)
  chives, snipped

Separate the sausages, arrange them on the grid of a grill pan and grill them slowly, turning them often until they are cooked and well browned. Drain them on kitchen paper and when cold, cut them into 1·25-cm (½-in) slices. Mix them with the red beans, onion, pepper and sweetcorn and toss in the vinaigrette. Sprinkle with the parsley and chives to serve.

Serves 8

Salmon Puffs

shortcrust pastry (see
  page 67)
225 g (8 oz) salmon,
  cooked
salt and pepper
60 ml (4 tablespoons)
  double cream

30 ml (2 tablespoons)
  tomato paste
15 ml (1 level tablespoon)
  parsley, chopped
oil for deep frying

Make the shortcrust pastry, using 250 g (10 oz) flour, 50 g (2 oz) margarine and 75 g (3 oz) lard. Roll it out and cut it into sixteen 10-cm (4-in) circles. Flake the cooked salmon finely and mix it with a little salt and plenty of pepper, the cream, tomato paste and parsley. Divide this mixture between the pastry rounds. Moisten the edges with a little water and fold over. Press the edges to seal, then decorate them by pressing with the back of a fork. Heat the oil until a cube of bread will brown in 1 minute, then fry the puffs, a few at a time, until they are golden and the pastry is well risen. Drain on kitchen paper and allow to cool before wrapping for a picnic.

Serves 8

Scotch Eggs

4 hard-boiled eggs, shelled
plain flour
salt and pepper
225 g (8 oz) sausagemeat
Worcestershire sauce

1 large egg, beaten
100 g (4 oz) breadcrumbs,
   toasted
oil for deep frying

Dry the eggs with kitchen paper, then season some flour with salt and pepper and use to dust the eggs. Break down the sausagemeat with a fork and season it with salt, pepper and a few drops of Worcestershire sauce. Divide it into four and mould one piece round each egg, keeping it an even thinness and keeping a good egg shape. Try not to have any creases in the sausagemeat and join it smoothly. Dip each one in beaten egg, then in the breadcrumbs to coat, patting them on well, then shaking off the excess. Heat the oil until a cube of bread browns in 1 minute and fry the eggs, two at a time, for about 8 minutes. Fry them slowly to ensure the sausagemeat cooks right through. Drain on kitchen paper, allow to cool and then wrap for a picnic.

Serves 4

Brownies

200 g (7 oz) caster sugar
50 g (2 oz) cocoa
75 g (3 oz) butter, melted
2 standard eggs, beaten
75 g (3 oz) plain flour

pinch of salt
5 ml (1 teaspoon) vanilla
  essence
50 g (2 oz) walnuts,
  chopped

Mix the caster sugar and cocoa and stir them into the cooled butter. Beat in the eggs and stir in the flour, salt, vanilla essence and walnuts. Turn the mixture into a greased 18-cm (7-in) square tin and bake at 160°C (325°F)/Gas 3 for 35 minutes or until a knife comes out clean. Leave them to cool in the tin for 10 minutes, then cut the brownie mixture into 9 squares.

Makes 9

Brandied Liver Pâté

0·75 kg (1½ lb) lamb's liver
225 g (8 oz) unsmoked
  bacon pieces, chopped
225 g (8 oz) pork belly
100 g (4 oz) chicken livers
1 clove garlic, crushed
salt and pepper

1 large egg, beaten
60 ml (4 tablespoons)
  double cream
60 ml (4 tablespoons)
  brandy
3 ml (½ level teaspoon)
  ground cardamom

Mince the lamb's liver, bacon pieces, pork belly and chicken livers once. Stir in the garlic, salt and pepper, egg, double cream and brandy. Season with ground cardamom. Spoon the mixture into an ovenproof dish, one suitable for carrying, and stand the dish in a meat tin full of water. Cover the pâté with a piece of foil and bake it at 160°C (325°F)/Gas 3 for about 2 hours. Allow it to cool, then cover the surface of the pâté with a small plate and put a weight on top. Leave it overnight. Either cut into slices and put on bread or take the whole dish to a picnic and serve it there.

Serves 8

Jellied Veal Pie

1 kg (2 lb) pie veal, cubed
salt
1 large onion, sliced
1 large carrot, sliced
2 sprigs of thyme
1 blade of mace

12 peppercorns
1 pig's trotter or piece of
   marrow bone
shortcrust pastry (see
   page 67)
pepper

Rinse the veal and put it in a large saucepan with a good pinch of salt, the onion, carrot, thyme, mace and peppercorns. Rinse the trotter or marrow bone and add it to the pan with 500 ml (1 pint) cold water. Bring to the boil slowly, then lower the heat, cover the pan and simmer for 2 hours. Remove the veal on to a plate and let it cool. Strain the stock and return it to the rinsed pan with the trotter or marrow bone and boil it until it is reduced to about 125 ml ($\frac{1}{4}$ pint).

Roll out half the pastry on a lightly-floured board and use to line a 25-cm (10-in) pie plate. Season the veal with salt and pepper and arrange it on the pastry. Moisten the pastry edge with water. Roll the remaining pastry and use to cover the pie. Press the edges to seal them, then trim and decorate. Make a good hole in the centre of the pie and bake it at 200°C (400°F)/Gas 6 for 25–35 minutes or until the pastry is golden brown.

Pour the strained stock through the hole in the top crust and leave it to cool completely, when the stock will have set to a jelly.

Serves 8

Preserves

The summer jams and jellies are the most luscious of the year. They are always the most expensive to buy yet because many of the soft fruits are particularly low in acid and pectin, these jams and jellies have got a bad reputation as being difficult and time-consuming to make. I believe this is unjust, for they more than repay the fraction of extra care required. Here are recipes for strawberry and raspberry jams, redcurrant jelly to serve with lamb and herb jellies made with an apple base to serve with all your roasts and cold meat.

The big pickling and chutney-making season has not yet arrived, but during the summer months you should make your tomato ketchup and red tomato chutneys. Sweetcorn makes a good pickle and, combined with those other summer fruits, the red and green peppers, a very attractive one. Marrow is most versatile. Besides making a good chutney, and a quick one too, by virtue of its delicate flavour marrow makes a lovely jam. I've flavoured my jam with ginger.

Now that the freezer plays a big part in our lives, we

should all experiment with freezer jams. I've given one recipe for strawberries but other fruits may be prepared in the same way and there are many advantages. There's a greater yield per kilo (2 lb) of fruit used and the time taken to prepare these jams is much less than that required for the more conventional methods. There's no cooking and as most of the fruits suitable for this method need processing during some of our hottest weather, this is a bonus. Finally, there's nothing to beat these jams for their real, fresh fruity taste. Try making redcurrant, raspberry, blackcurrant, logan-berry and peach freezer jams as well as the strawberry.

Whole Strawberry Jam

1·5 kg (3 lb) small firm strawberries, hulled
1·5 kg (3 lb) preserving sugar

juice of 2 large lemons, strained

Rinse the strawberries only if absolutely necessary and gently dry them on kitchen paper. Put them with the sugar in a preserving pan and heat it very gently until the sugar has dissolved. Add the lemon juice, bring quickly to the boil and boil rapidly for about 20 minutes. Test for a set by removing the pan from the heat, putting a small amount of jam on a plate and cooling it quickly in the fridge. It will wrinkle when you push the jam with your finger if setting point has been reached.

Pour into clean heated jam jars, cover with waxed discs and cellophane circles, label and store the jam in a cool, dark place.

Makes about 2·25 kg (5 lb)

Raspberry Jam

2·25 kg (5 lb) raspberries,   juice of 1 lemon,
2·25 kg (5 lb) preserving   strained
  sugar

Hull the raspberries, wash them only if really necessary, and put them in a preserving pan. Heat gently until the fruit softens and the juice begins to run. Add the sugar and lemon juice and continue to heat gently, stirring until the sugar has dissolved. Bring to the boil rapidly and boil for about 5 minutes or until setting point is reached. Pour into clean, warm jars, cover and label.

Makes about 3·5 kg (8 lb)

Blackcurrant Jam

2 kg (4 lb) blackcurrants,   3 kg (6 lb) preserving sugar
  cleaned

Put the fruit with 1·5 litres (3 pints) cold water in a large pan and simmer until the fruit is very soft and the contents of the pan have reduced a lot. Check a few of the currants to make sure the skins are tender and if not simmer until they are. Stir in the sugar and heat gently, stirring, until the sugar has dissolved. Bring to the boil quickly and boil hard until setting point is reached. Stir and pour into clean warm jars, cover and label.

Makes about 4½ kg (10 lb)

Marrow Jam

1·5 kg (3 lb) marrow,   juice of 3 lemons, strained
  prepared   25 g (1 oz) root ginger
1·5 kg (3 lb) preserving
  sugar

Weigh the marrow after removing the peel and seeds. Cut the flesh into cubes, put them in the top of a steamer and steam them until they are just tender – this should take about 15 minutes. Transfer the marrow to a large bowl and sprinkle with the sugar and lemon juice. Leave it overnight. Next day, pour the mixture into a preserving pan. Bruise the root ginger by walloping it with your rolling pin several times, then tie it in a small piece of muslin and add to the pan. Cook gently until the marrow is soft and transparent and the jam very syrupy. Remove the ginger, pour the jam into clean, warm jars, cover and label.

Makes about 2 kg (4 lb)

Apricot Jam

2 kg (4 lb) apricots, stoned   2 kg (4 lb) preserving sugar
juice of 1 lemon, strained

Put the apricot halves in a large pan with 375 ml (¾ pint) cold water. Add the lemon juice. Crack a few of the apricot stones and remove the kernels and dip them in boiling water.

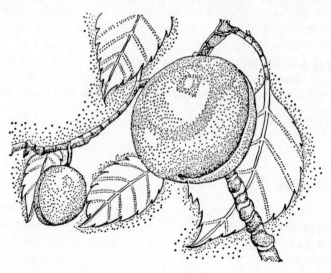

Remove and add to the pan and simmer the fruit until it is soft. Add the sugar, and heat gently to dissolve it, stirring often. Bring to the boil quickly and boil rapidly for about 15 minutes or until a set is reached. Stir and pour into clean warm jars and cover and label.

Makes about 3 kg (6 lb)

Peach Conserve

2 kg (4 lb) peaches,
  skinned

juice of 2 large lemons,
  strained
1 kg (2 lb) preserving sugar

Chop the peaches and put them in a large pan with 250 ml ($\frac{1}{2}$ pint) cold water and the lemon juice. Simmer the fruit until it is very soft and the contents of the pan are well reduced. Stir in the sugar and heat gently, stirring all the time, until the sugar has dissolved. Bring to a rapid boil and boil hard until setting point is reached. Stir and pour into clean, warm jars and cover and label. Keep this jam in the fridge because of its low sugar content. Though the jam has a marvellous flavour, full and fruity, if kept in a cupboard it will eventually ferment.

Makes about 2 kg (4$\frac{1}{2}$ lb)

Freezer Strawberry Jam

1 kg (2 lb) strawberries,
  hulled
1·75 kg (3$\frac{1}{2}$ lb) caster sugar

60 ml (4 tablespoons)
  lemon juice, strained
227 ml (1 bottle)
  commercial pectin

Halve the strawberries and put them in layers in a large bowl, sprinkling each layer as you prepare it with the caster sugar and lemon juice. Leave undisturbed until the sugar has completely dissolved. Stir well and add the commercial pectin, stirring until it begins to set. Pour into plastic containers with airtight seals, add the lids and label. Freeze and store in the freezer for no longer than six months. This makes a softer jam than usual—a cross between a sauce and a jam.

Makes about 2.75 kg (6 lb)

Redcurrant Jelly

2·5 kg (6 lb) redcurrants   preserving sugar

Wash the fruit but don't take the berries off the stalks. Put the fruit in a large pan with 1 litre (2 pints) cold water and simmer gently for about 40 minutes until the currants are really soft and squashy. Tie two or three layers of clean muslin to the legs of an upturned stool or chair and put a large bowl underneath the bag that's been formed. Pour the fruit and juice through the muslin and let it drip. Don't try to push it through because this will give you a cloudy jelly. If you have time, you can return the pulp to the pan with another 250 ml ($\frac{1}{2}$ pint) cold water and simmer the mixture again and pour it through the muslin. Mix the two lots of juice if you do this, then measure it and return it to the cleaned pan.

Add 450 g (1 lb) preserving sugar for every 600 ml (1 pint) juice in the pan and heat it slowly, stirring until the sugar has dissolved. Bring rapidly to the boil, then boil until setting point has been reached. Pour into clean, warm jars, cover and label.

Makes about 2 kg (4 lb)

Apple Mint Jelly

2 kg (4 lb) cooking apples,   60 ml (4 tablespoons)
   roughly chopped   lemon juice, strained
preserving sugar   6 sprigs of fresh mint

There is no need to peel or core the apples for this recipe,
just remove any bruised parts. Put the apples in a large pan
with 1 litre (1¾ pints) cold water and simmer the fruit until it
is really soft. Break down the fruit with a wooden spoon
while it cooks. Pour the pulp and juice through 3 layers of
muslin tied to the legs of an upturned chair or stool and let
it drip into a bowl underneath without disturbing it. You
can leave it to drip overnight, but be sure to cover it with
tea towels. Measure the juice back into the cleaned pan and
for every 600 ml (1 pint) juice, stir in 450 g (1 lb) sugar. Add
the lemon juice and the mint sprigs. Heat gently, stirring,
until the sugar has dissolved, then boil rapidly until setting
point is reached. Remove the mint sprigs and pour the jelly
into clean, warm jars and cover and label.

Makes about 1·5 kg (3½ lb)

Rosemary Jelly

Make the jelly in exactly the same way as the Apple Mint
Jelly but only add three 15-cm (6-in) sprigs of rosemary
because rosemary has a much stronger flavour than mint.

Thyme Jelly

Make the jelly in exactly the same way as the Apple Mint
Jelly but add 12 good sprigs of thyme or lemon thyme to the
apple juice instead of the mint sprigs.

Sweetcorn Pickle

225 g (½ lb) white cabbage, chopped
225 g (½ lb) celery, chopped
2 large red peppers, chopped
1 kg (2 lb) sweetcorn kernels (see page 13)
225 g (½ lb) granulated sugar
15 ml (1 level tablespoon) mustard powder
15 ml (1 level tablespoon) salt
15 ml (1 level tablespoon) pepper
1 litre (1¾ pints) white vinegar

Put the cabbage, celery and peppers in a large pan. (You can use a mixture of red and green peppers or all green; it depends on what's available and how you want the finished pickle to look.) Cook them together with 250 ml (½ pint) cold water for 30 minutes, then pour off any water and add the sweetcorn kernels. Add the sugar, mustard, salt, pepper and vinegar and mix well, then bring slowly to the boil and cook for about 30–40 minutes or until the vegetables are tender and the mixture reduced by about one third. Pour into clean, warm jars and cover with circles cut from cloth tied on with string. Seal them by brushing the cloth and string with melted candle wax. Once opened, keep the jars in the fridge; otherwise store them in a cool, dark cupboard.

Makes about 1·5 kg (3½ lb)

Tomato Chutney

2·5 kg (6 lb) tomatoes, skinned
0·5 kg (1 lb) cooking apples, chopped
0·5 kg (1 lb) onions, chopped
2 large carrots, chopped
0·5 kg (1 lb) Demerara sugar
15 g (½ oz) ground ginger
5 ml (1 level teaspoon) Cayenne pepper
15 ml (1 level tablespoon) salt
500 ml (1 pint) malt vinegar

Chop the tomatoes roughly and mix in a large pan with the apples, onions, carrots, sugar, ginger, Cayenne pepper, salt and vinegar. Bring to the boil then simmer, uncovered, for 1–1½ hours or until the mixture is thick. Pour into clean warm jars, cover and seal as described for Sweetcorn Pickle.

Makes about 2 kg (4 lb)

Tomato Ketchup

1·5 kg (3 lb) ripe tomatoes
1 small onion, chopped
1 large clove garlic, crushed
1 small green pepper, chopped
125 ml (¼ pint) white vinegar
5 ml (1 level teaspoon) salt
5 ml (1 level teaspoon) pepper
5 ml (1 level teaspoon) paprika
45 ml (3 tablespoons) lemon juice, strained
5 g (2 oz) granulated sugar

Chop the tomatoes and put them in a preserving pan and the onion, garlic and green pepper. Add the seeds of the green pepper to this recipe – they will add a touch more spiciness to the finished ketchup. Cook the mixture slowly until the onion is soft, then add the remaining ingredients and continue to cook slowly until the mixture is thick and soft and the consistency is even and without any obvious pieces of vegetable. Push the mixture through a sieve or blend it to a smooth pulp and then sieve it.

Sterilise some old ketchup bottles by boiling them, with their screw caps, for 15 minutes. Pour the ketchup through a funnel into the dried bottles and screw on the caps. Turn them back a half turn and sterilise the bottles again by putting them on a thick wad of newspaper in a pan deep enough for the water to come to the necks of the bottles. Put newspaper between the bottles to prevent them touching each other and the sides of the pan. Pour in water to the necks and above the level of the ketchup in the bottles. Bring to the boil and simmer for 30 minutes; if you have a thermometer, maintain the temperature at 77°C (170°F) for 30 minutes. Use an oven glove to remove the bottles on to a wooden board and tighten the screw caps.

Leave them until they are quite cold, then dip the caps and bottle necks in melted candle wax to ensure an airtight seal. Store your ketchup in a cool dark place and it will keep very well for months, but once opened, store it in the fridge and use it fairly quickly.

Makes about 700 ml (1¼ pints)

Marrow Chutney

2 kg (4 lb) marrow, cubed
75 g (3 oz) salt
1 kg (2 lb) cooking apples, chopped
0·5 kg (1 lb) small onions, skinned
2·5-cm (1-in) piece root ginger
6 chilli peppers
6 peppercorns
0·5 kg (1 lb) granulated sugar
1·5 litres (3 pints) malt vinegar

Layer the marrow in a large bowl, sprinkling each layer with salt. Next day, wash off the salt and put the marrow in a large pan with the apples and whole onions. Bash the ginger with a rolling pin several times and add it to the pan with the chilli peppers and peppercorns all tied up in a small piece of muslin. Cook for 15 minutes or until the marrow is soft. Add the sugar and vinegar and heat gently, stirring, until the sugar has dissolved, then bring the mixture to the boil. Cook for 15–20 minutes or until the chutney is thick. Remove the muslin bag and pour the chutney into clean warm jars, cover and seal as described for Sweetcorn Pickle.

Makes about 2.75 kg (6 lb)

Index

Almonds, Trout with, 62
Apple(s)
  Mint Jelly, 159
  Toffee, 123
Apricot, 97
  Fizzer, 127
  Fruit Cream, 100
  Jam, 156
  Marshmallow, 104
  Suédoise, 105
Artichoke(s), Globe, 9, 32
  Hearts, 32
  Mushroom Hearts, 37
  Salad, 34
  Spinach Stuffed, 18
  Stuffed, 17
  Vinaigrette, 16
Aubergines, 9, 78
  Baked Cheesy, 27
  Fried, 26
  Imam Bayouldi, 28
  Moussaka, 95
Avocado, 43, 97
  Guacamole, 147
  Iced, Soup, 48
  in June Fool, 109
  Pudding, 110
  Salad, 32
  Savoury Mousse, 54
  Vinaigrette, 52

Baked Cheesy Aubergines, 27
Baked Tomatoes, 9, 22
Bananas, Spicy, 142
Barbecues, 137–52
  Baked Fruits, 147
  Daubing Sauce, 145

Bazaars, 113–25
  see also individual sweets
  and Biscuits
Beans, Broad, 10–11, 36
Beans, Runner, 24–5, 33
Bean Salad Starter, 33
Beef, Potted, 79, 85
Beetroot Soup, 45
Biscuits, 113–14
  Brandy Snaps, 117
  Coconut Crisps, 119
  Florentines, 120
  Gingerbread Men, 114
  Gingernuts, 116
  Macaroons, 116
  Shrewsbury, 119
  Viennese Cookies, 115
Bisques, 43, 50–52
Blackcurrant, 154
  Jam, 155
Blue Trout, 58, 61
Borage, 126
Brandade de Saumon, 54
Brandied Liver Pâté, 151
Brandy Snaps, 117
Bread
  Cheesy Herb, 141
  for Sandwiches, 138
  Garlic, 140
Broad Beans, 9, 10, 32
  Salad, 36
  with Herb Butter, 11
  with Parsley Sauce, 11
Brownies, 151
Buffet Lunch, 79
Butter
  for Sandwiches, 138
  Herb, 11

Caribbean Shake, 129
Chaudfroid, Chicken, 79, 92
Cheese (*see overleaf*)

Cake, 98
  Herb Bread, 141
  Pork, 86
  Strawberry, Cake, 107
Cherries, 43, 97
  Clafouti, 103
  Fool, 109
  Ripe, 127
  Soup, 46–7
Chicken, 32, 79
  Chaudfroid, 92
  Galantine of, 88
  in a Basket, 91
  Strawberry, Salad, 42
  Sweet and Sour Drumsticks, 147
Chick Peas, Pounded, 43
Chilled Watercress Soup, 48
Chinese Spare Ribs, 94
Chive Sauce, for Runner Beans, 25
Chocolate
  Fudge, 125
  Ice Cream, 100
  Nutties, 121
Chutney, 153–4
  Marrow, 162
  Tomato, 160
Cider Apple Cup, 131
Clafouti, Cherry, 103
Coconut
  Crisps, 119
  Ice, 120
Coeur à la Crème, 97–8, 111–12
Coffee
  Iced, 133
  Irish, 132
  Turkish, 133
Cold Cucumber Soup, 47
Cold Sausage Salad, 149
Cold Sorrel Soup, 45
Cookies, Viennese, 115
Corn
  and Mushroom Quiche, 148

Corn – *contd.*
　Fritters, 13
　on the Cob, 9, 12–13
　Salad, 34
　Soufflé, 13
　Sweet, 32
Coulibiac, 65
Crab, 58
　Bisque, 43, 51
Cream Cheese Sweets, 97
Creamed Mushrooms on Toast, 29
Cricket Teas, 137
Croûtons, 43
Cucumber
　Cold, Soup, 47
　Mint Raita, 32, 36
Currant
　Sorbet, 101
　Soufflé, 106
Curried Prawns, 76
Cushions, Sole, 69
Cutlets in Pastry, 79, 95

Dover Sole, 58, 69
Dressed Crab, 60
Dressed Lobster, 59
Drinks, 126–36
　see also individual drinks
Drumsticks, Sweet and Sour Chicken, 147

Eggs, Scotch, 150

Fillings for Sandwiches, 138
First Courses, 43–52
　see also individual first courses
Fish, 32, 58–77
　Salad, 37
　see also individual fish
Florentines, 120
Fools, 97
　Cherry, 109
　June, 109

Freezer, 153
  Strawberry Jam, 157
Fricassee of Veal, 90
Fried Aubergines, 26
Fried Plaice, 71
Fritters
  Corn, 13
  Mushroom, 30
Fruit(s), 97–112, 126
  Crush, 134
  see also individual fruits
Fruit and Nut Fudge, 124
Fruity Crunch, 41
Fudge, 114
  Chocolate, 125
  Fruit and Nut, 124
  Vanilla, 124

Galantine, Chicken, 88
Gammon, Glazed, 86
Garlic Bread, 140
Gazpacho, 43, 49
Ginger, 153
  Beer, 126–8
  Bread Men, 114
  Flapjacks, 117
  Mint, 126
  Nuts, 116
Glazed Gammon, 86
Glazed Salmon, 63
Globe Artichokes, 9
Gooseberries, in June Fool, 109
Goujons, 48, 70
Grapefruit and Shrimp Salad, 39
Greek Fish Salad, 32, 37
Green Peppers, 9
  Mix, 35
  Soup, 44
Grilled Red Mullet, 73
Guacamole, 147

Halibut, 58

Halibut – *contd.*
  Mornay, 74
Ham, 78
  in Vol-au-Vents, 87
  Raised Veal and Ham Pie, 81
Hamburgers, 142
Herb Butter, 9, 11
  Jelly, 153
Hollandaise Sauce for Salmon, 64
Honeycomb Toffee, 122
Hummus, 43, 56

Ice, Raspberry Water, 98
Ice Cream
  Chocolate, 100
  Raspberry, Soda, 135
  Rich Vanilla, 99
  Sodas, 126
Iced Avocado Soup, 48
Iced Coffee, 133
Iced Orange Tea, 135
Imam Bayouldi, 9, 28
Irish Coffee, 132

Jam, 153–4
  Apricot, 156
  Blackcurrant, 155
  Freezer Strawberry, 157
  Marrow, 155
  Raspberry, 155
  Whole Strawberry, 154
Jellied Veal Pie, 152
Jelly, 153
  Apple Mint, 159
  Redcurrant, 158
  Rosemary, 159
  Thyme, 159
June Fool, 109

Kassandra, Runner Beans, 25
Kebabs
  Lamb, 143

Lamb Tikka, 143
Ketchup, 161
Kir, 129

Lamb
 Cutlets in Pastry Jackets, 95
 Kebabs, 143
 Tikka Kebabs, 143
Leeks, 43
Lemon
 Balm, 126
 Butter, 67
 Sauce with, Marrow, 15
 Thyme, 126
Lettuce, 32
Liver, Brandied, Pâté, 151
Loaf, Veal, 84
Lobster, 58
 Bisque, 43, 50
 Dressed, 59
Loganberry, 154
Lovage, 126

Macaroons, 116
Marinated Mushrooms, 35
Marrow, 9, 78, 153
 Chutney, 162
 Jam, 155
 Perfectly Cooked, 14
 Smothered, 15
 Stuffed, 84
 with Lemon Sauce, 15
Marshmallow, Apricot, 97
Meat, 78–96
 see also individual meats
Meunière, Dover Sole, 69
Milk Shakes, 126
 Strawberry, 133
Mint Cream, 101
 Tea, 136
Minty Cooler, 134
Mornay, Halibut, 74

Moussaka, 78, 95
Mousse, 97
  Avocado Savoury, 54
  Salmon, 55
Mullet, Red, 58, 73
Mushroom(s), 32
  Artichoke Hearts, 37
  Corn and, Quiche, 148
  Creamed, on Toast, 29
  Creamed Soup, 146
  Fritters, 30
  Marinated, 35
  Tartlets, 30
Mustard sauce, 15

Olive Oil, 10
Orange
  Drinks, 126
  Iced, Tea, 135
Orangeade, 135

Parcel, Red Mullet in, 73
Parsley Sauce, 11
Pâté, Brandied Liver, 151
Pavlova, Raspberry, 103
Peach(es), 97, 154
  and Redcurrant Dreams, 104
  Conserve, 157
  in White Wine, 102
  Salad, 38
Peanut Brittle, 122
Peperonata, 9, 20
Pepper(s) Green and Red, 9, 32, 78, 153
  Mix, 35
  Soup, 44
  Stuffed, 21
Peppermint Creams, 114, 121
Perfectly Cooked Marrow, 14
Picnics, 137–52
Pie, Jellied Veal, 152
Pineapple
  Barbeque Sauce, 144

Mint, 126
Plaice, 58
  Fried, 71
  Goujons, 70
  in Seafood Timbales, 72
Pork
  Cheese, 86
  Chinese Spare Ribs, 94
Potatoes, 43
Potted Beef, 79, 85
Potted Shrimps, 43, 53
Poultry Vol-au-Vents, 87
Prawns
  Curried, 76
  in Sour Cream, 75
Preserves, 153–62
  see also individual preserves
Pressed Tongue, 79
Pudding(s)
  Avocado, 110
  Summer, 111

Quiche, Corn and Mushroom, 148

Radishes, 32
Raspberry(ies), 97, 153
  Ice Cream Soda, 135
  Jam, 155
  Pavlova, 103
  Water Ice, 98
Ratatouille, 9, 19
Redcurrant, 153
  and Peach Dreams, 104
  Jelly, 158
Redhot Sauce, 145
Red Mullet, 58
  Grilled, 73
  in a Parcel, 73
Red Peppers, 9
Rich Vanilla Ice Cream, 99
Rosemary Jelly, 159

Runner Beans, 9, 24, 32
  Kassandra, 25
  Salad Starter, 33
  with Chive Sauce, 25

Salade Niçoise, 32, 39
Salads, 32–43
  see also individual salads
Salmon
  Brandade de, 54
  Coulibiac, 65
  Glazed, 63
  Mousse, 55
  Puffs, 149
  Salad, 41
  Tourte, 67
  Trout, 58, 63
  with Hollandaise Sauce, 64
Sandwiches, Super, 138–40
Sangria, 128
Sauce(s)
  Barbecue, 144
  Béchamel, 30
  Chive, 25
  Fruity, 97
  Hollandaise, 64
  Lemon, 15
  Mustard, 15
  Parsley, 11
  Redhot, 145
  Tartare, 70
  Sweet and Sour, 147
Sausage
  Cold Salad, 149
  Meat Patties, 141
Scotch Eggs, 150
Seafood Timbales, 72
Shortbread, 118
Shrewsbury Biscuits, 119
Shrimp
  and Grapefruit Salad, 39
  Potted, 43, 53

Smoked Cod's Roe, 43
Smothered Marrow, 15
Sole
  Cushions, 69
  Dover, 58
  Meunière, 69
  Véronique, 68
Sorbet, Currant, 101
Sorrel, 43
  Cold Soup, 45
Soufflés, 97
  Corn, 13
Soups, 43–52, 146–7
  see also individual soups
Sour Cream, Prawns in, 75
Spare Ribs, Chinese, 94
Spearmint, 126
Spicy Bananas, 142
Spinach Stuffed Artichokes, 18
Starters, 43–57
  see also individual starters
Strawberry(ies), 97, 153
  Cheesecake, 107
  Chicken Salad, 42
  Ice Cream, 99
  Jam, Whole, 154
  Milk Shake, 133
Stuffed Artichokes, 17
Stuffed Marrow, 84
Stuffed Peppers, 21
Stuffed Tomatoes, 23
Suédoise, Apricot, 105
Summer Pudding, 111
Sunshine Stinger, 131
Super Sandwiches, 138
Sweet and Sour Chicken Drumsticks, 147
Sweetcorn, 32, 153
  Pickle, 160

Tagliatelle Napoletana, 21
Tahini, 56
Taramasalata, 43, 53

Tartare Sauce, 70
Tartlets, Mushroom, 30
Thyme Jelly, 159
Timbales, Seafood, 72
Toffee Apples, 123
Tomato(es), 9, 43, 88, 153
    Bake, 9, 22
    Chutney, 160
    for Sandwiches, 138
    Ices, 43, 52
    Ketchup, 161
    Salad, 36
    Soup, 44
    Stuffed, 32
    Stuffed, Turkish Style, 93
Tongue, Pressed, 80
Tourte, Salmon, 67
Trout, 58
    with Almonds, 62
    see also blue trout and salmon trout
Turkey, 87
Turkish Coffee, 133
Turkish Style, Stuffed Tomatoes, 93

Vanilla Fudge, 124
Vanilla Ice Cream, Rich, 99
Veal, 78
    Fricassée of, 90
    in Soured Cream, 81
    Jellied, Pie, 152
    Loaf, 84
    Raised, and Ham Pie, 81
    Vitello Tonnato, 79
    Wiener Schnitzel, 83
Vegetables, 9–32, 43
    see also individual vegetables
Véronique, Sole, 68
Vichyssoise, 43, 46
Viennese Cookies, 115
Vinaigrette, 16
Vitello Tonnato, 79
Vol-au-Vents, 79, 87

Watercress, 43
   Chilled, Soup, 48
Wedding Special, 130
Wiener Schnitzel, 78, 83